The World of the Incas

The World of the Incas

by
William H. Prescott

A Pierre Waleffe Book

Minerva

Contents

*The photographs reproduced in this book were
made by* **H. and J. Roger-Viollet**
with the exception of three color plates.

Printed by Istituto Italiano d'Arti Grafiche, Bergamo

"The empire of Peru stretched along the Pacific"—Pachacamac beach, seen from the Temple of the Sun.

1 - Physical aspect of the country - Sources of Peruvian Civilization - Empire of the Incas - Royal Family - Nobility.

Of the numerous nations which occupied the great American continent at the time of its discovery by the Europeans, the two most advanced in power and refinement were undoubtedly those of Mexico and Peru. But, though resembling one another in extent of civilization, they differed widely as to the nature of it; and the philosophical student of his species may feel a natural curiosity to trace the different steps by which these two nations strove to emerge from the state of barbarism, and place themselves on a higher point in the scale of humanity.—In a former

work I have endeavored to exhibit the institutions and character of the ancient Mexicans, and the story of their conquest by the Spaniards. The present will be devoted to the Peruvians; and, if their history shall be found to present less strange anomalies and striking contrasts than that of the Aztecs, it may interest us quite as much by the pleasing picture it offers of a well-regulated government and sober habits of industry under the patriarchal sway of the Incas.

The empire of Peru, at the period of the Spanish invasion, stretched along the Pacific from about the second degree north to the thirty-seventh degree of south latitude; a line, also, which describes the western boundaries of the modern republics of Ecuador, Peru, Bolivia, and Chili. Its breadth cannot so easily be determined; for, though bounded

5

everywhere by the great ocean on the west, towards the east it spread out, in many parts, considerably beyond the mountains, to the confines of barbarous states, whose exact position is undetermined, or whose names are effaced from the map of history. It is certain, however, that its breadth was altogether disproportioned to its length.

The topographical aspect of the country is very remarkable. A strip of land, rarely exceeding twenty leagues in width, runs along the coast, and is hemmed in through its whole extent by a colossal range of mountains, which, advancing from the Straits of Magellan, reaches its highest elevation—indeed, the highest on the American continent—about the seventeenth degree south, and, after crossing the line, gradually subsides into hills of inconsiderable magnitude, as it enters the Isthmus of Panama. This is the famous Cordillera of the Andes, or "copper mountains", as termed by the natives, though they might with more reason have been called "mountains of gold". Arranged sometimes in a single line, though more frequently in two or three lines running parallel or obliquely to each other, they seem to the voyager on the ocean but one continuous chain; while the huge volcanoes, which to the inhabitants of the table-land look like solitary and independent masses, appear to him only like so many peaks of the same vast and magnificent range. So immense is the scale on which Nature works in these regions, that it is only when viewed from a great distance, that the spectator can, in any degree, comprehend the relation of the several parts to the stupendous whole. Few of the works of Nature, indeed, are calculated to produce impressions of higher sublimity than the aspect of this coast, as it is gradually unfolded to the eye of the mariner sailing on the distant waters of the Pacific; where mountain is seen to rise above mountain, and Chimborazo, with its glorious canopy of snow, glittering far above the clouds, crowns the whole as with a diadem.

"A colossal range of mountains, the famous Cordillera of the Andes... Mountain is seen to rise above mountain, and Chimborazo, with its glorious canopy of snow, crowns the whole". — Right, the llama, the "Peruvian sheep".

The face of the country would appear to be peculiarly unfavorable to the purposes both of agriculture and of internal communication. The sandy strip along the coast, where rain never falls, is fed only by a few scanty streams, that furnish a remarkable contrast to the vast volumes of water which roll down the eastern sides of the Cordilleras into the Atlantic. The precipitous steeps of the sierra, with its splintered sides of porphyry and granite, and its higher regions wrapped in snows that never melt under the fierce sun of the equator, unless it be from the desolating action of its own volcanic fires, might seem equally unpropitious to the labors of the husbandman. And all communication between the parts of the long-extended territory might be thought to be precluded by the savage character of the region, broken up by precipices, furious torrents, and impassable *quebradas*—those hideous rents in the mountain chain, whose depths the eye of the terrified traveller, as he winds along his aërial pathway, vainly endeavors to fathom. Yet the industry, we might almost say, the genius, of the Indian was sufficient to overcome all these impediments of Nature.

By a judicious system of canals and subterraneous aqueducts, the waste places on the coast were refreshed by copious streams, that clothed them in fertility and beauty. Terraces were raised upon the steep sides of the Cordillera; and, as the different elevations had the effect of difference of latitude, they exhibited in regular gradation every variety of vegetable form, from the stimulated growth of the tropics, to the temperate products of a northern clime; while flocks of *llamas*—the Peruvian sheep—wandered with their shepherds over the broad, snow-covered wastes on the crests of the sierra, which rose beyond the limits of cultivation. An industrious population settled along the lofty regions of the plateaus, and towns and hamlets, clustering amidst orchards and widespreading gardens, seemed suspended in the air far above the ordinary elevation of the clouds. Intercourse was maintained between these numerous settlements by means of great roads which traversed the mountain passes, and opened an easy communication between the capital and the remotest extremities of the empire.

The source of this civilization is traced to the valley of Cuzco, the central region of Peru, as its name implies. The origin of the Peruvian empire, like the origin of all nations, except the very few which, like our own, have had the good fortune to date from a civilized period and people, is lost in the mists of fable, which, in fact, have settled as darkly round its history as round that of any nation, ancient or modern, in the Old World. According to the tradition most familiar to the European scholar, the time was, when the ancient races of the continent were all plunged in deplorable barbarism; when they worshipped nearly every object in nature indiscriminately; made war their pastime, and feasted on the flesh of their slaughtered captives. The Sun, the great luminary and parent of mankind, taking compassion on their degraded condition, sent two of his children, Manco Capac and Mama Oello Huaco, to gather the natives into communities, and teach them the arts of civilized life. The celestial pair, brother and sister, husband and wife, advanced along the high plains in the neighborhood of Lake Titicaca, to about the sixteenth degree south. They bore with them a golden wedge, and were directed to take up their residence on the spot where the sacred emblem should without effort sink into the ground. They proceeded accordingly but a short distance, as far as the valley of Cuzco, the spot indicated by the performance of the miracle, since there the wedge speedily sank into the earth and disappeared for ever. Here the children of the Sun

Above : "The savage character of the region..."— "The source of this civilization is traced to the valley of Cuzco"
Right : the site of the city, as it was seen from the palace of the Inca : "The worthy metropolis of a great and flourishing monarchy"...

8

established their residence, and soon entered upon their beneficent mission among the rude inhabitants of the country; Manco Capac teaching the men the arts of agriculture, and Mama Oello initiating her own sex in the mysteries of weaving and spinning. The simple people lent a willing ear to the messengers of Heaven, and, gathering together in considerable numbers, laid the foundations of the city of Cuzco. The same wise and benevolent maxims, which regulated the conduct of the first Incas, descended to their successors, and under their mild sceptre a community gradually extended itself along the broad surface of the table-land, which asserted its superiority over the surrounding tribes. Such is the pleasing picture of the origin of the Peruvian monarchy, as portrayed by Garcilasso de la Vega, the descendant of the Incas, and through him made familiar to the European reader.

But this tradition is only one of several current among the Peruvian Indians, and probably not the one most generally received. Another legend speaks of certain white and bearded men, who, advancing from the shores of Lake Titicaca, established an ascen-

dency over the natives, and imparted to them the blessings of civilization. It may remind us of the tradition existing among the Aztecs in respect to Quetzalcoatl, the good deity, who with a similar garb and aspect came up the great plateau from the east on a like benevolent mission to the natives. The analogy is the more remarkable, as there is no trace of any communication with, or even knowledge of, each other to be found in the two nations.

The date usually assigned for these extraordinary events was about four hundred years before the coming of the Spaniards, or early in the twelfth century. But, however pleasing to the imagination, and however popular, the legend of Manco Capac, it requires but little reflection to show its improbability, even when divested of supernatural accompaniments. On the shores of Lake Titicaca extensive ruins exist at the present day, which the Peruvians themselves acknowledge to be of older date than the pretended advent of the Incas, and to have furnished them with the models of their architecture. The date of their appearance, indeed, is manifestly irreconcilable with their subsequent history. No account assigns to the Inca dynasty more than thirteen princes before the Conquest. But this number is altogether too small to have spread over four hundred years, and would not carry back the foundations of the monarchy, on any probable computation, beyond two centuries and a half,—an antiquity not incredible in itself, and which, it may be remarked, does not precede by more than half a century the alleged foundation of the capital of Mexico. The fiction of Manco Capac and his sister-wife was devised, no doubt, at a later period, to gratify the vanity of the Peruvian monarchs, and to give additional sanction to their authority by deriving it from a celestial origin.

We may reasonably conclude that there existed in the country a race advanced in civilization before the time of the Incas; and, in conformity with nearly every tradition, we may derive this race from the neighborhood of Lake Titicaca; a conclusion strongly confirmed by the imposing architectural remains which still endure, after the lapse of so many years, on its borders. Who this race were, and whence they came, may afford a tempting theme for inquiry to the speculative antiquarian. But it is a land of darkness that lies far beyond the domain of history.

The same mists that hang round the origin of the Incas continue to settle on their subsequent annals; and, so imperfect were the records employed by the Peruvians, and so confused and contradictory their traditions, that the historian finds no firm footing on which to stand till within a century of the Spanish conquest. At first, the progress of the Peruvians seems to have been slow, and almost imperceptible. By their wise and temperate policy, they gradually won over the neighboring tribes to their dominion, as these latter became more and more convinced of the benefits of a just and well-regulated government. As they grew stronger, they

"The imposing architectural remains which still endure on the shores of Lake Titicaca"...

were enabled to rely more directly on force; but, still advancing under cover of the same beneficent pretexts employed by their predecessors, they proclaimed peace and civilization at the point of the sword. The rude nations of the country, without any principle of cohesion among themselves, fell one after another before the victorious arm of the Incas. Yet it was not till the middle of the fifteenth century that the famous Topa Inca Yupanqui, grandfather of the monarch who occupied the throne at the coming of the Spaniards, led his armies across the terrible desert of Atacama, and, penetrating to the southern region of Chili, fixed the permanent boundary of his dominions at the river Maule. His son, Huayna Capac, possessed of ambition and military talent fully equal to his father's, marched along the Cordillera towards the north, and, pushing his conquests across the equator, added the powerful kingdom of Quito to the empire of Peru.

The ancient city of Cuzco, meanwhile, had been gradually advancing in wealth and population, till it had become the worthy metropolis of a great and flourishing monarchy. It stood in a beautiful valley on an elevated region of the plateau, which, among the Alps, would have been buried in eternal snows, but which within the tropics enjoyed a genial and salubrious temperature. Towards the north it was defended by a lofty eminence, a spur of the great Cordillera; and the city was traversed by a river, or rather a small stream, over which bridges of timber, covered with heavy slabs of stone, furnished an easy means of communication with the opposite banks. The streets were long and narrow; the houses low, and those of the poorer sort built of clay and reeds. But Cuzco was the royal residence, and was adorned with the ample dwellings of the great nobility; and the massy fragments still incorporated in many of the modern edifices bear testi-

"The famous Topa Inca Yupanqui (above), grandfather of the monarch who occupied the throne at the coming of the Spaniards...". His son, Huayna Capac (below).

In Cuzco: "Towards the north rose a strong fortress". Two views of its ruins—"The fortress consisted of three towers, one (of which) was appropriated to the Inca". Right: look-out post.

mony to the size and solidity of the ancient.

The health of the city was promoted by spacious openings and squares, in which a numerous population from the capital and the distant country assembled to celebrate the high festivals of their religion. For Cuzco was the "Holy City"; and the great temple of the Sun, to which pilgrims resorted from the furthest borders of the empire, was the most magnificent structure in the New World, and unsurpassed, probably, in the costliness of its decorations by any building in the Old.

Towards the north, on the sierra or rugged eminence already noticed, rose a strong fortress, the remains of which at the present day, by their vast size, excite the admiration of the traveller. It was defended by a single wall of great thickness, and twelve hundred feet long on the side facing the city, where the precipitous character of the ground was of itself almost sufficient for its defense. On the other quarter, where the approaches were less difficult, it was protected by two other semicircular walls of the same length as the preceding. They were separated, a considerable distance from one another and from the fortress; and the intervening ground was raised so that the walls afforded a breastwork for the troops stationed there in times of assault. The fortress consisted of three towers, detached from one another. One was appropriated to the Inca, and was garnished with the sumptuous decorations befitting a royal residence, rather than a military post. The other two were held by the garrison, drawn from the Peruvian nobles, and commanded by an officer of the blood royal; for the position was of too great importance to be intrusted to inferior hands. The hill was excavated below the towers, and several subterraneous galleries communicated with the city and the palaces of the Inca.

The fortress, the walls, and the galleries were all built of stone, the heavy blocks of which were not laid in regular courses, but so

disposed that the small ones might fill up the interstices between the great. They formed a sort of rustic work, being rough-hewn except towards the edges, which were finely wrought; and, though no cement was used, the several blocks were adjusted with so much exactness and united so closely, that it was impossible to introduce even the blade of a knife between them. Many of these stones were of vast size; some of them being full thirty-eight feet long, by eighteen broad, and six feet thick.

We are filled with astonishment, when we consider, that these enormous masses were hewn from their native bed and fashioned into shape, by a people ignorant of the use of iron; that they were brought from quarries, from four to fifteen leagues distant, without the aid of beasts of burden; were transported across rivers and ravines, raised to their elevated position on the sierra, and finally adjusted there with the nicest accuracy, without the knowledge of tools and machinery familiar to the European. Twenty thousand men are said to have been employed on this great structure, and fifty years consumed in the building. However this may be, we see in it the workings of a despotism which had the lives and fortunes of its vassals at its absolute disposal, and which, however mild in its general character, esteemed these vassals, when employed in its service, as lightly as the brute animals for which they served as a substitute.

The fortress of Cuzco was but part of a system of fortifications established throughout their dominions by the Incas. This system formed a prominent feature in their military policy; but before entering on this latter, it will be proper to give the reader some view of their civil institutions and scheme of government.

The sceptre of the Incas, if we may credit their historian, descended in unbroken succession from father to son, through their whole

Left: stairs leading to the second terrace of the Inca fortress of Cuzco. "We are filled with astonishment, when we consider, that these enormous masses were hewn from their native bed and fashioned into shape, by a people ignorant of the use of iron; that they were transported, without the aid of beasts of burden, across ravines... Twenty thousand men are said to have been employed on this great structure". According to the picture below, due, like many others reproduced in this book, to a close descendant of the Incas, the nobles themselves took part in the building of this huge work.

15

dynasty. Whatever we may think of this, it appears probable that the right of inheritance might be claimed by the eldest son of the *Coya,* or lawful queen, as she was styled, to distinguish her from the host of concubines who shared the affections of the sovereign. The queen was further distinguished, at least in later reigns, by the circumstance of being selected from the sisters of the Inca, an arrangement which, however revolting to the ideas of civilized nations, was recommended to the Peruvians by its securing an heir to the crown of the pure heaven-born race, uncontaminated by any mixture of earthly mould.

In his early years, the royal offspring was intrusted to the care of the *amautas,* or "wise men", as the teachers of Peruvian science were called, who instructed him in such elements of knowledge as they possessed, and especially in the cumbrous ceremonial of their religion, in which he was to take a prominent part. Great care was also bestowed

"The Coya, *or lawful queen": the old print below presents the sovereign attended by her hairdresser.*

on his military education, of the last importance in a state which, with its professions of peace and good-will, was ever at war for the acquisition of empire.

In this military school he was educated with such of the Inca nobles as were nearly of his own age; for the sacred name of Inca—a fruitful source of obscurity in their annals—was applied indifferently to all who descended by the male line from the founder of the monarchy. At the age of sixteen the pupils underwent a public examination, previous to their admission to what may be called the order of chivalry. This examination was conducted by some of the oldest and most illustrious Incas. The candidates were required to show their prowess in the athletic exercices of the warrior; in wrestling and boxing, in running such long courses as fully tried their agility and strength, in severe fasts of several days' duration, and in mimic combats, which although the weapons were blunted, were always attended with wounds, and sometimes with death. During this trial, which lasted thirty days, the royal neophyte fared no better than his comrades, sleeping on the bare ground, going unshod, and wearing a mean attire,—a mode of life, it was supposed, which might tend to inspire him with more sympathy with the destitute. With all this show of impartiality, however, it will probably be doing no injustice to the judges to suppose that a politic discretion may have somewhat quickened their perceptions of the real merits of the heir-apparent.

At the end of the appointed time, the candidates selected as worthy of the honors of their barbaric chivalry were presented to the sovereign, who condescended to take a principal part in the ceremony of inauguration. He began with a brief discourse, in which, after congratulating the young aspirants on the proficiency they had shown in martial exercises, he reminded them of the responsibilities attached to their birth and station; and, addressing them affectionately as "children of the Sun", he exhorted them to imitate their great progenitor in his glorious career of beneficence to mankind. The novices then drew near, and, kneeling one by one before the Inca, he pierced their ears with a golden bodkin; and this was suffered to remain there till an opening had been made large enough for the enormous pendants which were peculiar to their order, and which gave them, with the Spaniards, the name of *orejones*. This ornament was so massy in the ears of the sovereign, that the cartilage was distended by it nearly to the shoulder, producing what seemed a monstrous deformity in the eyes of the Europeans, though, under the magical influence of fashion, it was regarded as a beauty by the natives.

When this operation was performed, one of the most venerable of the nobles dressed the feet of the candidates in the sandals worn by the order, which may remind us of the ceremony of buckling on the spurs of the Christian knight. They were then allowed to assume the girdle or sash around the loins, corresponding with the *toga virilis* of the Romans, and intimating that they had reached the season of manhood. Their heads were adorned with garlands of flowers, which, by their various colors, were emblematic of the clemency and goodness that should grace the character of every true warrior; and the leaves of an evergreen plant were mingled with the flowers, to show that these virtues should endure without end. The prince's head was further ornamented by a fillet, or tasselled fringe, of a yellow color, made of the fine threads of the vicuña wool, which encircled the forehead as the peculiar insignia of the heir apparent. The great body of the Inca nobility next made their appearance, and, beginning with those nearest of kin, knelt down before the prince, and did him homage as

"The enormous pendants peculiar to the order of the Incas, which gave them, with the Spaniards, the name of *orejones*". (above) "The sandals worn by the order" (below).

successor to the crown. The whole assembly then moved to the great square of the capital, where songs, and dances, and other public festivities closed the important ceremonial of the *huaracu*.

The reader will be less surprised by the resemblance which this ceremonial bears to the inauguration of a Christian knight in the feudal ages, if he reflects that a similar analogy may be traced in the institutions of other people more or less civilized; and that it is natural that nations, occupied with the one great business of war, should mark the period, when the preparatory education for it was ended, by similar characteristic ceremonies.

Having thus honorably passed through his ordeal, the heir-apparent was deemed worthy to sit in the councils of his father, and was employed in offices of trust at home, or, more usually, sent on distant expeditions to practise in the field the lessons which he had hitherto studied only in the mimic theatre of war. His first campaigns were conducted under the renowned commanders who had grown grey in the service of his father; until, advancing in years and experience, he was placed in command himself, and, like Huayna Capac, the last and most illustrious of his line, carried the banner of the rainbow, the armorial ensign of his house, far over borders, among the remotest tribes of the plateau.

The government of Peru was a despotism, mild in its character, but in its form a pure and unmitigated despotism. The sovereign was placed at an immeasurable distance above his subjects. Even the proudest of the Inca nobility, claiming a descent from the same divine original as himself, could not venture into the royal presence, unless barefoot, and bearing a light burden on his shoulders in token of homage. As the representative of the Sun, he stood at the head of the priesthood, and presided at the most important of the religious festivals. He raised armies, and usually commanded them in person. He imposed taxes, made laws, and provided for their execution by the appointment of judges, whom he removed at pleasure. He was the source from which every thing flowed,—all dignity, all power, all emolument. He was, in short, in the well-known phrase of the European despot, "himself the state".

The Inca asserted his claims as a superior being by assuming a pomp in his manner of living well calculated to impose on his people. His dress was of the finest wool of the vicuña, richly dyed, and ornamented with a profusion of gold and precious stones. Round his head was wreathed a turban of many-colored folds, called the *llautu;* and a tasselled fringe, like that worn by the prince, but of a scarlet color, with two feathers of a rare and curious bird, called the *coraquenque,* placed upright in it, were the distinguishing insignia of royalty. The birds from which these feathers were obtained were found in a desert country among the mountains; and it was death to destroy or to take them, as they were reserved for the exclusive purpose of supplying the royal head-gear. Every succeeding monarch was provided with a new pair of these plumes, and his credulous subjects fondly believed that only two individuals of the species had ever existed to furnish the simple ornament for the diadem of the Incas.

Although the Peruvian monarch was raised so far above the highest of his subjects, he condescended to mingle occasionally with them, and took great pains personally to inspect the condition of the humbler classes. He presided at some of the religious celebrations, and on these occasions entertained the great nobles at his table, when he complimented them, after the fashion of more civilized nations, by drinking the health of those whom he most delighted to honor.

But the most effectual means taken by the Incas for communicating with their people

"Round the head (of the Inca) was wreathed a turban of many-colored folds, with two feathers of a rare bird" (above)—To be compared with the head-dress of a chief (below).

19

cleuan alynga los yris callaua

"The sedan, or litter, in which (the Incas) travelled, richly emblazoned with gold and emeralds, was guarded by a numerous escort".

were their progresses through the empire. These were conducted, at intervals of several years, with great stade and magnificence. The sedan, or litter, in which they travelled, richly emblazoned with gold and emeralds, was guarded by a numerous escort. The men who bore it on their shoulders were provided by two cities, specially appointed for the purpose. It was a post to be coveted by no one, if, as is asserted, a fall was punished by death. They travelled with ease and expedition, halting at the *tambos,* or inns, erected by government along the route, and occasionally at the royal palaces, which in the great towns afforded ample accommodations to the whole of the monarch's retinue. The noble roads which traversed the table-land were lined with people, who swept away the stones and stubble from their surface, strewing them with sweet-scented flowers, and vying with each other in carrying forward the baggage from one village to another. The monarch halted from time to time to listen to the grievances of his subjects, or to settle some points which had been referred to his decision by the regular tribunals. As the princely train wound its way along the mountain passes, every place was thronged with spectators eager to catch a glimpse of their sovereign; and, when he raised the curtains of his litter, and showed himself to their eyes, the air was rent with acclamations as they invoked blessings on his head. Tradition long commemorated the spots at which he halted, and the simple people of the country held them in reverence as places consecrated by the presence of an Inca.

The royal palaces were on a magnificent scale, and, far from being confined to the capital or a few principal towns, were scattered over all the provinces of their vast empire. The buildings were low, but covered a wide extent of ground. Some of the apartments were spacious, but they were generally small, and had no communication with one another, except that they opened into a common square or court. The walls were made of blocks of stone of various sizes, like those described in the fortress of Cuzco, rough-hewn, but carefully wrought near the line of junction, which was scarcely visible to the eye. The roofs were of wood or rushes, which have perished under the rude touch of time, that has shown more respect for the walls of the edifices. The whole seems to have been characterized by solidity and strength, rather than by any attempt at architectural elegance.

But whatever want of elegance there may have been in the exterior of the imperial dwellings, it was amply compensated by the interior, in which all the opulence of the Peruvian princes was ostentatiously displayed. The sides of the apartments were thickly studded with gold and silver ornaments. Niches, prepared in the walls, were filled with images of animals and plants curiously wrought of the same costly materials; and even much of the domestic furniture, including the ustensils devoted to the most ordinary menial services, displayed the like wanton magnificence! With these gorgeous decora-

"The sides of the apartments were thickly studded with gold and silver ornaments"—These birds decorate a plate of gold in repoussé work.

"... With these gorgeous decorations were mingled richly colored stuffs of the delicate manufacture of the Peruvian wool.".

tions were mingled richly colored stuffs of the delicate manufacture of the Peruvian wool, which were of so beautiful a texture, that the Spanish sovereigns, with all the luxuries of Europe and Asia at their command, did not disdain to use them. The royal household consisted of a throng of menials, supplied by the neighboring towns and villages, which, as in Mexico, were bound to furnish the monarch with fuel and other necessaries for the consumption of the palace.

But the favorite residence of the Incas was at Yucay, about four leagues distant from the capital. In this delicious valley, locked up within the friendly arms of the sierra, which sheltered it from the rude breezes of the east, and refreshed by gushing fountains and streams of running water, they built the most beautiful of their palaces. Here, when wearied with the dust and toil of the city, they loved

Bathing was one of the Incas' great pleasures. We can still see in the ruins of some buildings of the time small bathrooms with running water, like this one, with benches and holes for the utensils.

to retreat, and solace themselves with the society of their favorite concubines, wandering amidst groves and airy gardens, that shed around their soft, intoxicating odors, and lulled the senses to voluptuous repose. Here, too, they loved to indulge in the luxury of their baths, replenished by streams of crystal water which were conducted through subterraneous silver channels into basins of gold. The spacious gardens were stocked with numerous varieties of plants and flowers that grew without effort in this *temperate* region of the tropics, while parterres of a more extraordinary kind were planted by their side, glowing with the various forms of vegetable life skilfully imitated in gold and silver! Among them the Indian corn, the most beautiful of American grains, is particularly commemorated, and the curious workmanship is noticed with which the golden ear was half

23

disclosed amidst the broad leaves of silver, and the light tassel of the same material that floated gracefully from its top.

If this dazzling picture staggers the faith of the reader, he may reflect that the Peruvian mountains teemed with gold; that the natives understood the art of working the mines, to a considerable extent; that none of the ore, as we shall see hereafter, was converted into coin, and that the whole of it passed into the hands of the sovereign for his own exclusive benefit, whether for purposes of utility or ornament. Certain it is that no fact is better attested by the Conquerors themselves, who had ample means of information, and no motive for misstatement.—The Italian poets, in their gorgeous pictures of the gardens of Alcina and Morgana, came nearer the truth than they imagined.

Our surprise, however, may reasonably be excited, when we consider that the wealth displayed by the Peruvian princes was only that which each had amassed individually for himself. He owed nothing to inheritance from his predecessors. On the decease of an Inca, his palaces were abandoned, all his treasures, except what were employed in his obsequies, his furniture and apparel, were suffered to remain as he left them, and his mansions, save one, were closed up for ever. The new sovereign was to provide himself with every thing new for his royal state. The reason of this was the popular belief, that the soul of the departed monarch would return after a time to reänimate his body on earth; and they wished that he should find every thing to which he had been used in life prepared for his reception.

When an Inca died, or, to use his own language, "was called home to the mansions of his father, the Sun", his obsequies were celebrated with great pomp and solemnity. The bowels were taken from the body, and deposited in the temple of Tampu, about five leagues from the capital. A quantity of his plate and jewels was buried with them, and a number of his attendants and favorite concubines, amounting sometimes, it is said, to a thousand, were immolated on his tomb. Some of them showed the natural repugnance to the sacrifice occasionally manifested by the victims of a similar superstition in India. But these were probably the menials and more humble attendants; since the women have been known, in more than one instance, to lay violent hands on themselves, when restrained from testifying their fidelity by this act of conjugal martyrdom. This melancholy ceremony was followed by a general mourning throughout the empire. At stated intervals, for a year, the people assembled to renew the expressions of their sorrow, processions were made, displaying the banner of the departed monarch; bards and minstrels were appointed to chronicle his achievements, and their songs continued to be rehearsed at high festivals in the presence of the reigning monarch,—thus stimulating the living by the glorious example of the dead.

The body of the deceased Inca was skilfully embalmed, and removed to the great temple of the Sun at Cuzco. There the Peruvian sovereign, on entering the awful sanctuary, might behold the effigies of his royal ancestors, ranged in opposite files,—the men on the right, and their queens on the left, of the great luminary which blazed in refulgent gold on the walls of the temple. The bodies, clothed in the princely attire which they had been accustomed to wear, were placed on chairs of gold, and sat with their heads inclined downward, their hands placidly crossed over their bosoms, their countenances exhibiting their natural dusky hue,—less liable to change than the fresher coloring of a European complexion—and their hair of raven black, or silvered over with age, according to the period at which they died! It seemed like a company

The hemicycle of the great temple of Cuzco.

of solemn worshippers fixed in devotion,—so true were the forms and lineaments to life. The Peruvians were as successful as the Egyptians in the miserable attempt to perpetuate the existence of the body beyond the limits assigned to it by nature.

They cherished a still stranger illusion in the attentions which they continued to pay to these insensible remains, as if they were instinct with life. One of the houses belonging to a deceased Inca was kept open and occupied by his guard and attendants, with all the state appropriate to royalty. On certain festivals, the revered bodies of the sovereigns were brought out with great ceremony into the public square of the capital. Invitations were sent by the captains of the guard of the respective Incas to the different nobles and officers of the court; and entertainments were provided in the names of their masters, which displayed all the profuse magnificence of their treasures,—and "such a display" says an ancient chronicler, "was there in the great square of Cuzco, on this occasion, of gold and silver plate and jewels, as no other city in the world ever witnessed". The banquet was served by the menials of the respective households, and the guests partook of the melancholy cheer in the presence of the royal phantom with the same attention to the forms of courtly etiquette as if the living monarch had presided!

The nobility of Peru consisted of two orders, the first and by far the most important of which was that of the Incas, who, boasting a common descent with their sovereign, lived, as it were, in the reflected light of his glory. As the Peruvian monarchs availed themselves of the right of polygamy to a very liberal extent, leaving behind them families of one or even two hundred children, the nobles of the blood royal, though comprehending only their descendants in the male line, came in the course of years to be very numerous. They

Left: the amphitheatre of sacrifices in the temple of Huaca-Kenko near Cuzco.

Below: The Inca surrounded by nobles.

It is interesting to compare this head of an Inca chief (left) with the picture below showing a couple of Peruvian peasants of to-day; the features have not changed.

were divided into different lineages, each of which traced its pedigree to a different member of the royal dynasty, though all terminated in the divine founder of the empire.

They were distinguished by many exclusive and very important privileges; they wore a peculiar dress; spoke a dialect, if we may believe the chronicler, peculiar to themselves, and had the choicest portion of the public domain assigned for their support. They lived, most of them, at court, near the person of the prince, sharing in his counsels, dining at his board, or supplied from his table. They alone were admissible to the great offices in the priesthood. They were invested with the command of armies, and of distant garrisons, were placed over the provinces, and, in short, filled every station of high trust and emolument. Even the laws, severe in their general tenor, seem not to have been framed with reference to them; and the people, investing the whole order with a portion of the sacred character which belonged to the sovereign, held that an Inca noble was incapable of crime.

The other order of nobility was the *Curacas,* the caciques of the conquered nations, or their descendants. They were usually continued by the government in their places, though they were required to visit the capital occasionally, and to allow their sons to be educated there as the pledges of their loyalty. It is not easy to define the nature or extent of their privileges. They were possessed of more or less power, according to the extent of their patrimony, and the number of their vassals. Their authority was usually transmitted from father to son, though sometimes the successor was chosen by the people. They did not occupy the highest posts of state, cr those nearest the person of the sovereign, like the nobles of the blood. Their authority seems to have been usually local.

It was the Inca nobility, indeed, who constituted the real strength of the Peruvian monarchy. Attached to their prince by ties of consanguinity, they had common sympathies and, to a considerable extent, common interests with him. Distinguished by a peculiar dress and insignia, as well as by language and blood, from the rest of the community, they were never confounded with the other tribes and nations who were incorporated into the great Peruvian monarchy. After the lapse of centuries, they still retained their individuality as a peculiar people. Clustering around the throne, they formed and invincible phalanx, to shield it alike from secret conspiracy and open insurrection. Though living chiefly in the capital, they were also distributed throughout the country in all its high stations and strong military posts, thus establishing lines of communication with the court, which enabled the sovereign to act simultaneously and with effect on the most distant quarters of his empire. They possessed, moreover, an intellectual preëminence, which no less than their station, gave them authority with the people. Indeed, it may be said to have been the principal foundation of their authority. The crania of the Inca race show a decided superiority over the other races of the land in intellectual power; and it cannot be denied that it was the fountain of that peculiar civilization and social polity, which raised the Peruvian monarchy above every other state in South America. Whence this remarkable race came, and what was its early history, are among those mysteries that meet us so frequently in the annals of the New World, and which time and the antiquary have as yet done little to explain.

An aspect of the remains of the Temple of the Sun at Pachacamac.

31

Left: this stele with figure, three foot three high, dates from the origins of the Inca civilization. It is believed that this civilization sprang in the neighbourhood of Lake Titicaca. (right).

2 - Orders of the State - Provisions for Justice - Division of lands - Revenues and registers - Great roads and posts - Military tactics and policy.

If we are surprised at the peculiar and original features of what may be called the Peruvian aristocracy, we shall be still more so as we descend to the lower orders of the community, and see the very artificial character of their institutions,—as artificial as those of ancient Sparta, and, though in a different way, quite as repugnant to the essential principles of our nature. The institutions of Lycurgus, however, were designed for a petty state, while those of Peru, although originally intended for such, seemed, like the magic tent in the Arabian tale, to have an indefinite power of expansion, and were as well suited to the most flourishing condition of the empire as to its infant fortunes. In this remarkable accommodation to change of circumstances we see the proofs of a contrivance that argues no slight advance in civilization.

The name of Peru was not known to the natives. It was given by the Spaniards, and originated, it is said, in a misapprehension of the Indian name of "river". However this may be, it is certain that the natives had no other epithet by which to designate the large collection of tribes and nations who were assembled under the sceptre of the Incas, than that of *Tavantinsuyu,* or "four quarters of the world". This will not surprise a citizen of the United States, who has no other name by which to class himself among nations than what is borrowed from a quarter of the globe. The kingdom, conformably to its name, was divided into four parts, distinguished each by a separate title, and to each of which ran one of the four great roads that diverged from

Numerous torrents give Peruvian nature one of its peculiar aspects.

CIVDAD
LAGRÃCIVDADICAVE

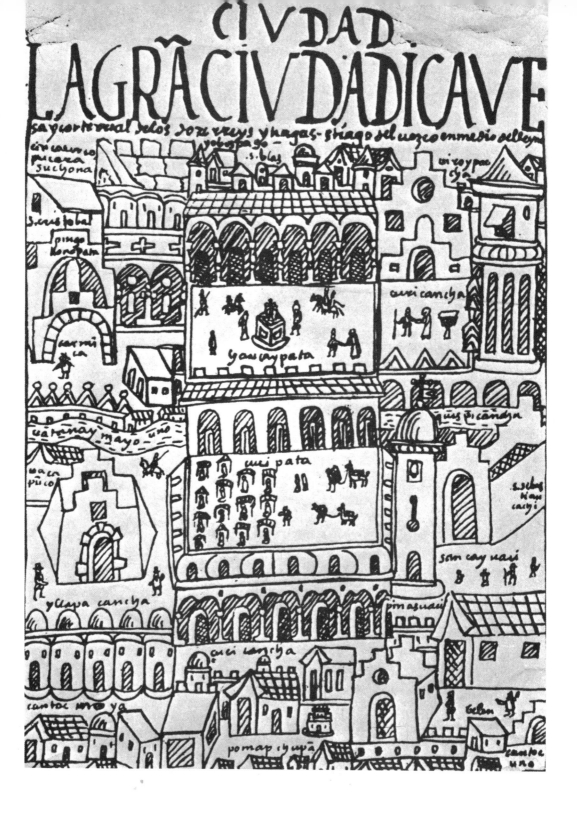

sa y corte real delos jncas reys y nacas · s.tiago del cuzco en medio del reyno

cir catuyo picasa suchona

s. bias

viracocha yya

s.cristobal

pisac koncon

cusi cancha

carmi ca

yauuaypata

cuis picancha

uatanay mayo uno

cuci pata

s.sebas tiaga cuzi

uaca pucol

soncay uaci

yllaua cancha

pina suaci

cuci cancha

cantoc uno yo

belun

pomap chupa

santoc uno

Cuzco, the capital or *navel* of the Peruvian monarchy. The city was in like manner divided into four quarters; and the various races, which gathered there from the distant parts of the empire, lived each in the quarter nearest to its respective province. They all continued to wear their peculiar national costume, so that it was easy to determine their origin; and the same order and system of arrangement prevailed in the motley population of the capital, as in the great provinces of the empire. The capital, in fact, was a miniature image of the empire.

The four great provinces were each placed under a viceroy or governor, who ruled over them with the assistance of one or more councils for the different departments. These viceroys resided, some portion of their time, at least, in the capital, where they constituted a sort of council of state to the Inca. The nation at large was distributed into decades, or small bodies of ten; and every tenth man, or head of a decade, had supervision of the rest,—being required to see that they enjoyed the rights and immunities to which they were entitled, to solicit aid in their behalf from government, when necessary, and to bring offenders to justice. To this last they were stimulated by a law that imposed on them, in case of neglect, the same penalty that would have been incurred by the guilty party. With this law hanging over his head, the magistrate of Peru, we may well believe, did not often go to sleep on his post.

Ruins of the Inca palace at Cuzco.—Left: this "view" of the capital is subsequent to the Spanish conquest but the central market-places existed already before the coming of the Conquistadors.

The people were still further divided into bodies of fifty, one hundred, five hundred, and a thousand, with each an officer having general supervision over those beneath, and the higher ones possessing, to a certain extent, authority in matters of police. Lastly, the whole empire was distributed into sections or departments of ten thousand inhabitants, with a governor over each, from the Inca nobility, who had control over the *curacas* and other territorial officers in the district. There were, also, regular tribunals of justice, consisting of magistrates in each of the towns or small communities, with jurisdiction over petty offences, while those of a graver character were carried before superior judges, usually the governors or rulers of the districts. These judge all held their authority and received their support from the Crown, by which they were appointed and removed at pleasure. They were obliged to determine every suit in five days from the time it was brought before them; and there was no appeal from one tribunal to another. Yet there were important provisions for the security of justice. A committee of visitors patrolled the kingdom at certain times to investigate the character and conduct of the magistrates; and any neglect or violation of duty was punished in the most exemplary manner. The inferior courts were also required to make monthly returns of their proceedings to the higher ones, and these made reports in like manner to the viceroys; so that the monarch, seated in the centre of his dominions, could look abroad, as it were, to the most distant extremities, and review and rectify any abuses in the administration of the law.

The laws were few and exceedingly severe. They related almost wholly to criminal matters. Few other laws were needed by a people who had no money, little trade, and hardly any thing that could be called fixed property. The crimes of theft, adultery, and murder were all capital; though it was wisely provided that some extenuating circumstances might be allowed to mitigate the punishment. Blasphemy against the Sun, and malediction of the Inca,—offences, indeed, of the same complexion,—were also punished with death. Removing landmarks, turning the water away from a neighbor's land into one's own, burning a house, were all severely punished. To burn a bridge was death. The Inca allowed no obstacle to those facilities of communication so essential to the maintenance of public order. A rebellious city or province was laid waste, and its inhabitants exterminated. Rebellion against the "Child of the Sun,", was the greatest of all crimes.

The simplicity and severity of the Peruvian code may be thought to infer a state of society but little advanced; which had few of those complex interests and relations that grow up in a civilized community, and which had not proceeded far enough in the science of legislation to economize human suffering by proportioning penalties to crimes. But the Peruvian institutions must be regarded from a different point of view from that in which we study those of other nations. The laws emanated from the sovereign, and that sovereign held a divine commission, and was possessed of a divine nature. To violate the law was not only to insult the majesty of the throne, but it was sacrilege. The slightest offence, viewed in this light, merited death; and the gravest could incur no heavier penalty. Yet, in the infliction of their punishments, they showed no unnecessary cruelty; and the sufferings of the victim were not prolonged by the ingenious torments so frequent among barbarous nations.

These legislative provisions may strike us as very defective, even as compared with those of the semi-civilized races of Anahuac, where a gradation of courts, moreover, with the right of appeal, afforded a tolerable security for

"The laws were few and exceedingly severe... The crimes of theft, adultery and murder were all capital".
Left: execution of a judgment condemning a nobleman to the loss of an eye; a man and a woman hanged (by the hair) for "guilty" intercourse.
Below: lapidation of an adulterous couple.

39

justice. But in a country like Peru, where few but criminal causes were known, the right of appeal was of less consequence. The law was simple, its application easy; and where the judge was honest, the case was as likely to be determined correctly on the first hearing as on the second. The inspection of the board of visitors, and the monthly returns of the tribunals, afforded no slight guaranty for their integrity. The law which required a decision within five days would seem little suited to the complex and embarrassing litigation of a modern tribunal. But, in the simple questions submitted to the Peruvian judge, delay would have been useless; and the Spaniards, familiar with the evils growing out of long-protracted suits, where the successful litigant is too often a ruined man, are loud in their encomiums of this swift-handed and economical justice.

The fiscal regulations of the Incas, and the laws respecting property, are the most remarkable features in the Peruvian polity. The whole territory of the empire was divided into three parts, one for the Sun, another for the Inca, and the last for the people. Which of the three was the largest is doubtful. The proportions differed materially in different provinces. The distribution, indeed, was made on the same general principle, as each new conquest was added to the monarchy; but the proportion varied according to the amount of population, and the greater or less amount of land consequently required for the support of the inhabitants.

The lands assigned to the Sun furnished a revenue to support the temples, and maintain the costly ceremonial of the Peruvian worship and the multitudinous priesthood. Those reserved for the Inca went to support the royal state, as well as the numerous members of his household and his kindred, and supplied the various exigencies of government. The remainder of the lands was divided, *per capita,* in equal shares among the people. It was

provided by law, as we shall see hereafter, that every Peruvian should marry at a certain age. When this event took place, the community or district in which he lived furnished him with a dwelling, which, as it was constructed of humble materials, was done at little cost. A lot of land was then assigned to him sufficient for his own maintenance and that of his wife. An additional portion was granted for every child, the amount allowed for a son being the double of that for a daughter. The division of the soil was renewed every year, and the possessions of the tenant were increased or diminished according to the numbers in his family. The same arrangement was observed with reference to the curacas, except only that a domain was assigned to them corresponding with the superior dignity of their stations.

A more thorough and effectual agrarian law than this cannot be imagined. In other countries where such a law has been introduced, its operation, after a time, has given way to the natural order of events, and, under the superior intelligence and thrift of some and the prodigality of others, the usual vicissitudes of fortune have been allowed to take their course, and restore things to their natural inequality. Even the iron law of Lycurgus ceased to operate after a time, and melted away before the spirit of luxury and avarice. The nearest approach to the Peruvian constitution was probably in Judea, where, on the recurrence of the great national jubilee, at the close of every half-century, estades reverted to their original proprietors. There was this important difference in Peru; that not only did the lease, if we may so call it, terminate with the year, but during that period the tenant had no power to alienate or to add to his possessions. The end of the brief term found him in precisely the same condition that he was in at the beginning. Such a state of things might be supposed to be fatal to any thing like attachment to the soil, or to

that desire of improving it, which is natural to the permanent proprietor, and hardly less so to the holder of a long lease. But the practical operation of the law seems to have been otherwise; and it is probable, that, under the influence of that love of order and aversion to change which marked the Peruvian institutions, each new partition of the soil usually confirmed the occupant in his possession, and the tenant for a year was converted into a proprietor for life.

The territory was cultivated wholly by the people. The lands belonging to the Sun were first attended to. They next tilled the lands of the old, of the sick, of the widow and the orphan, and of soldiers engaged in actual service; in short, of all that part of the community who, from bolidy infirmity or any other cause, were unable to attend to their own concerns. The people were then allowed to work on their own ground, each man for himself, but with the general obligation to assist his neighbor, when any circumstance—the burden of a young and numerous family, for example—might demand it. Lastly, they cultivated the lands of the Inca. This was done, with great ceremony, by the whole population in a body. At break of day, they were summoned together by proclamation from some neighboring tower or eminence, and all the inhabitants of the district, men, women, and children, appeared dressed in their gayest apparel, bedecked with their little store of finery and ornaments, as if for some

"The flocks of llamas were appropriated exclusively to the Sun and to the Inca".

great jubilee. They went through the labors of the day with the same joyous spirit, chanting their popular ballads which commemorated the heroic deeds of the Incas, regulating their movements by the measure of the chant, and all mingling in the chorus, of which the word *hailli*, or "triumph", was usually the burden. These national airs had something soft and pleasing in their character, that recommended them to the Spaniards; and many a Peruvian song was set to music by them after the Conquest, and was listened to by the unfortunate natives with melancholy satisfaction, as it called up recollections of the past, when their days glided peacefully away under the sceptre of the Incas.

A similar arrangement prevailed with respect to the different manufactures as to the agricultural products of the country. The flocks of llamas, or Peruvian sheep, were appropriated exclusively to the Sun and to the Inca. Their number was immense. They were scattered over the different provinces, chiefly in the colder regions of the country, where they were intrusted to the care of experienced shepherds, who conducted them to different pastures according to the change of season. A large number was every year sent to the capital for the consumption of the Court, and for the religious festivals and sacrifices. But these were only the males, as no female was allowed to be killed. The regulations for the care and breeding of these flocks were prescribed with the greatest minuteness, and with a sagacity which excited the admiration of the Spaniards, who were familiar with the management of the great migratory flocks of merinos in their own country.

At the appointed season, they were all sheared, and the wool was deposited in the public magazines. It was then dealt out to each family in such quantities as sufficed for its wants, and was consigned to the female part of the household, who were well instructed in the business of spinning and weaving. When this labor was accomplished, and the family was provided with a coarse but warm covering, suited to the cold climate of the mountains,—for, in the lower country, cotton, furnished in like manner by the Crown, took the place, to a certain extent, of wool,—the people were required to labor for the Inca. The quantity of the cloth needed, as well as the peculiar kind and quality of the fabric, was first determined at Cuzco. The work was then apportioned among the different provinces. Officers, appointed for the purpose, superintended the distribution of the wool, so that the manufacture of the different articles should be intrusted to the most competent hands. They did not leave the matter here,

"The joyous spirit of the popular ballads"...

43

puron runa

enest reyno delas yñs

PRIMERA CALLE
AVACOCVARMI

de edad de treynta y tres años

muger de tributo

"The wool was consigned to the female part of the household, who were well instructed in the business of spinning and weaving... In this domestic labor all the female part of the estabⅼishment was expected to join. Occupation was found for all, from the child five years old to the aged matron not too infirm to hold a distaff"... The picture above shows that the technique, even the designs of the weaving have not much changed ever since in some parts of Peru. The specimen on the right dates from the Inca period.

but entered the dwellings, from time to time, and saw that the work was faithfully executed. This domestic inquisition was not confined to the labors for the Inca. It included, also, those for the several families; and care was taken that each household should employ the materials furnished for its own use in the manner that was intended, so that no one should be unprovided with necessary apparel. In this domestic labor all the female part of the establishment was expected to join. Occupation was found for all, from the child five years old to the aged matron not too infirm to hold a distaff. No one, at least none but the decrepit and the sick, was allowed to eat the bread of idleness in Peru. Idleness was a crime in the eye of the law, and, as such, severely punished; while industry was publicly commended and stimulated by rewards.

The like course was pursued with reference to the other requisitions of the government. All the mines in the kingdom belonged to the Inca. They were wrought exclusively for his benefit, by persons familiar with this service, and selected from the districts where the mines were situated. Every Peruvian of the lower class was a husbandman, and, with the exception of those already specified, was expected to provide for his own support by the cultivation of his land. A small portion of the community, however, was instructed in mechanical arts; some of them of the more elegant kind, subservient to the purposes of luxury and ornament. The demand for these was chiefly limited to the sovereign and his Court; but the labor of a larger number of hands was exacted for the execution of the great public works which covered the land. The nature and amount of the services required were all determined at Cuzco by commissioners well instructed in the resources of the country, and in the character of the inhabitants of different provinces.

This information was obtained by an admir-

Right: a scraping tool from the age of the Incas. Above: transport of metal, from the famous illustrator of the Conquistadors, Th. de Bry.

"No one was allowed to eat the bread of idleness in Peru... Every Peruvian of the lower class was a husbandman". Even his wife had to help him in collecting potatoes and transporting them in bags, on the backs of the llamas, to the magazines of the provinces.

"... These (magazines) constructed of stone, were divided between the Sun and the Inca", who inspected them from time to time, as it can be seen in the picture on the right.

able regulation, which has scarcely a counterpart in the annals of a semi-civilized people. A register was kept of all the births and deaths throughout the country, and exact returns of the actual population were made to government every year, by means of the *quipus,* a curious invention, which will be explained hereafter. At certain intervals, also, a general survey of the country was made, exhibiting a complete view of the character of the soil, its fertility, the nature of its products, both agricultural and mineral,—in short, of all that constituted the physical resources of the empire. Furnished with these statistical details, it was easy for the government, after determining the amount of requisitions, to distribute the work among the respective provinces best qualified to execute it. The task of apportioning the labor was assigned to the local authorities, and great care was taken that is should be done in such a manner, that, while the most competent hands were selected, it should not fall disproportionately heavy on any.

The different provinces of the country furnished persons peculiarly suited to different employments, which, as we shall see hereafter, usually descended from father to son. Thus, one district supplied those most skilled in working the mines, another the most curious workers in metals, or in wood, and so on. The artisan was provided by government with the materials; and no one was required to give more than a stipulated portion of his time to the public service. He was then succeeded by another for the like term; and it should be observed, that all who were engaged in the employment of the government—and the remark applies equally to agricultural labor— were maintained, for the time, at the public expense. By this constant rotation of labor, it was intended that no one should be over-burdened, and that each man should have time to provide for the demands of his own house-

hold. It was impossible—in the judgment of a high Spanish authority—to improve on the system of distribution, so carefully was it accommodated to the condition and comfort of the artisan. The security of the working classes seems to have been ever kept in view in the regulations of the government; and these were so discreetly arranged, that the most wearing and unwholesome labors, as those of the mines, occasioned no detriment to the health of the laborer; a striking contrast to his subsequent condition under the Spanish rule.

A part of the agricultural produce and manufactures was transported to Cuzco, to minister to the immmediate demands of the Inca and his Court. But far the greater part was stored in magazines scattered over the different provinces. These spacious buildings, constructed of stone, were divided between the Sun and the Inca, though the greater share seems to have been appropriated by the monarch. By a wise regulation, any deficiency in the contributions of the Inca might be supplied from the granaries of the Sun. But

49

such a necessity could rarely have happened; and the providence of the government usually left a large surplus in the royal depositories, which was removed to a third class of magazines, whose design was to supply the people in seasons of scarcity, and occasionally, to furnish relief to individuals, whom sickness or misfortune had reduced to poverty; thus, in a manner, justifying the assertion of a Castilian document, that a large portion of the revenues of the Inca found its way back again, through one channel or another, into the hands of the people. These magazines were found by the Spaniards, on their arrival, stored with all the various products and manufactures of the country,—with maize, *coca, quinua,* woolen and cotton stuffs of the finest quality, with vases and utensils of gold, silver, and copper, in short, with every article of luxury or use within the compass of Peruvian skill. The magazines of grain, in particular, would frequently have sufficed for the consumption of the adjoining district for several years. An inventory of the various products of the country, and the quarters whence they were obtained, was every year taken by the royal officer, and recorded by the *quipucamayus* on their registers, with surprising regularity and precision. These registers were transmitted to the capital, and submitted to the Inca, who could thus at a glance, as it were, embrace the whole results of the national industry, and see how far they corresponded with the requisitions of government.

Such are some of the most remarkable features of the Peruvian institutions relating to property, as delineated by writers who, however contradictory in the details, have a general conformity of outline. These institutions are certainly so remarkable, that it is hardly credible they should ever have been enforced throughout a great empire, and for a long period of years. Yet we have the most unequivocal testimony to the fact from the

This vase presents a simple woman of ancient Peru with her baby (Museum of Chicago. Photo by Giraudon).

50

Spaniards, who landed in Peru in time to witness their operation; some of whom, men of high judicial station and character, were commissioned by the government to make investigations into the state of the country under its ancient rulers.

The impositions on the Peruvian people seem to have been sufficiently heavy. On them rested the whole burden of maintaining, not only their own order, but every other order in the state. The members of the royal house, the great nobles, even the public functionaries, and the numerous body of the priesthood, were all exempt from taxation. The whole duty of defraying the expenses of the government belonged to the people. Yet this was not materially different from the condition of things formerly existing in most parts of Europe, where the various privileged classes claimed exemption—not always with success, indeed—from bearing part of the public burdens. The great hardship in the case of the Peruvian was, that he could not add a rood to his own possessions, nor advance himself one hair's breadth in the social scale. The great and universal motive to honest industry, that of bettering one's lot, was lost upon him. The great law of human progress was not for him. As he was born, so he was to die. Even his time he could not properly call his own. Without money, with little properly of any kind, he paid his taxes in labor. No wonder that the government should have dealt with sloth as a crime. It was a crime against the state, and to be wasteful of time was, in a manner, to rob the exchequer. The Peruvian, laboring all his life for others, might be compared to the convict in a treadmill, going the same dull round of incessant toil, with the consciousness, that, however profitable the results to the state, they were nothing to him.

But this is the dark side of the picture. If no man could become rich in Peru, no man could become poor. No spendthrift could waste his

These children at the foot of the fortress of Sacsayhuaman, are lineally descended from the Inca race.

substance in riotous luxury. No adventurous schemer could impoverish his family by the spirit of speculation. The law was constantly directed to enforce a steady industry and a sober management of his affairs. No mendicant was tolerated in Peru. When a man was reduced by poverty or misfortune, (it could hardly be by fault,) the arm of the law was stretched out to minister relief; not the stinted relief of private charity, nor that which is doled out, drop by drop, as it were, from the frozen reservoirs of "the parish," but in generous measure, bringing no humiliation to the object of it, and placing him on a level with the rest of his countrymen.

No man could be rich, no man could be poor, in Peru; but all might enjoy, and did enjoy, a competence. Ambition, avarice, the love of change, the morbid spirit of discontent, those passions which most agitate the minds of men, found no place in the bosom of the Peruvian. The very condition of his being seemed to be at war with change. He moved on in the same unbroken circle in which his fathers had moved before him, and in which his children were to follow. It was the object of the Incas to infuse into their subjects a spirit of passive obedience and tranquillity, —a perfect acquiescence in the established order of things. In this they fully succeeded. The Spaniards who first visited the country are emphatic in their testimony, that no government could have been better suited to the genius of the people; and no people could have appeared more contented with their lot, or more devoted to their government.

Those who may distrust the accounts of Peruvian industry will find their doubts re-

"Remains of temples, palaces, fortresses, astonish the traveller by their number, the massive character of the materials, and the grandeur of the design." Numerous buildings have been erected in Cuzco upon Inca constructions still intact. (right).

54

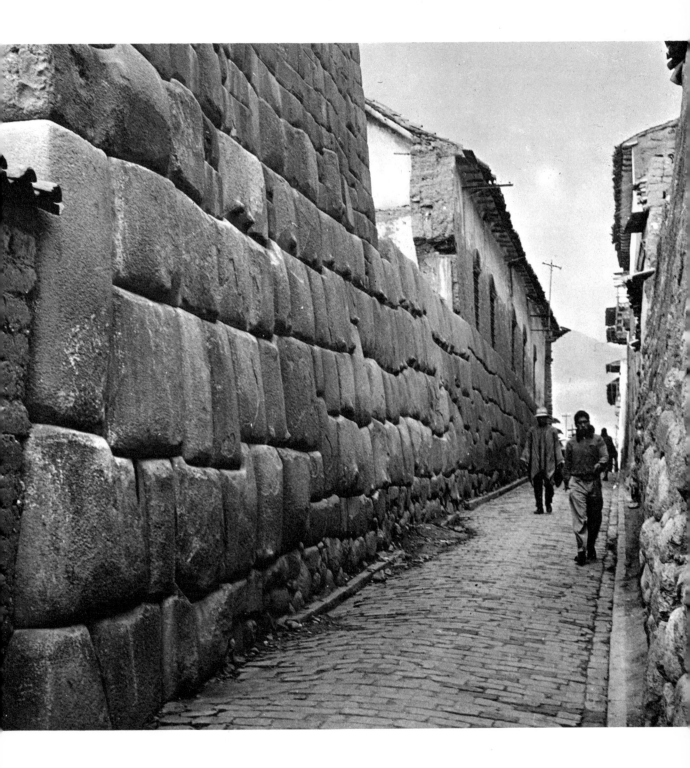

moved on a visit to the country. The traveller still meets, especially in the central regions of the table-land, with memorials of the past, remains of temples, palaces, fortresses, terraced mountains, great military roads, aqueducts, and other public works, which, watever degree of science they may display in their execution, astonish him by their number, the massive character of the materials, and the grandeur of the design. Among them, perhaps the most remarkable are the great roads, the broken remains of which are still in sufficient preservation to attest their former magnificence. There were many of these roads, traversing different parts of the kingdom; but the most considerable were the two which etended from Quito to Cuzco, and, again diverging from the capital, continued in a southern direction towards Chili.

One of these roads passed over the grand plateau, and the other along the lowlands on the borders of the ocean. The former was much the more difficult achievement, from the character of the country. It was conducted over pathless sierras buried in snow; galleries were cut for leagues through the living rock; rivers were crossed by means of bridges that swung suspended in the air; precipices were scaled by stairways hewn out of the native bed; ravines of hideous depth were filled up with solid masonry; in short, all the difficulties that beset a wild and mountainous region, and which might appall the most courageous engineer of modern times, were encountered and successfully overcome. The length of the road, of which scattered fragments only remain, is variously estimated, from fifteen hundred to two thousand miles; and stone pillars, in the manner of European milestones, were erected at stated intervals of some what more than a league, all along the route. Its breadth scarcely exceeded twenty feet. It was built of heavy flags of freestone, and in some parts, at least, covered with a bituminous

Above: a street of Pachacamac.
"... Over some of the boldest streams it was necessary to construct suspension bridges, made of the tough fibres of the maguey, *or of the osier of the country... woven into cables of the thickness of a man's body" (Right).*

56

cement, which time has made harder than the stone itself. In some places, where the ravines had been filled up with masonry, the mountain torrents, wearing on it for ages, have gradually eaten a way through the base, and left the superincumbent mass—such is the cohesion of the materials—still spanning the valley like an arch.

Over some of the boldest streams it was necessary to construct suspension bridges, as they are termed, made of the tough fibres of the maguey, or of the osier of the country, which has an extraordinary degree of tenacity and strength. These osiers were woven into cables of the thickness of a man's body. The huge ropes, then stretched across the water, were conducted through rings or holes cut in immense buttresses of stone raised on the opposite banks of the river, and there secured to heavy pieces of timber. Several of these enormous cables, bound together, formed a bridge, which, covered with planks, well secured and defended by a railing of the same osier materials on the sides, afforded a sage passage for the traveller. The length of this aërial bridge, sometimes exceeding two hundred feet, caused it, confined, as it was, only at the extremities, to dip with an alarming inclination towards the centre, while the motion given to it by the passenger occasioned an oscillation still more frightful, as his eye wandered over the dark abyss of waters that foamed and tumbled many a fathom beneath. Yet these light and fragile fabrics were crossed without fear by the Peruvians, and are still retained by the Spaniards over those streams which, from the depth or impetuosity of the current, would seem impraticable for the usual modes of conveyance. The wider and more tranquil waters were crossed on *balsas*— a kind of raft still much used by the natives— to which sails were attached, furnishing the only instance of this higher kind of navigation among the American Indians.

Left: this boat made of maguey *from the shores of Lake Titicaca is exactly similar to the boats of the Inca period.*

"Among the works (of the Incas), the most remarkable are perhaps the great roads".— "All along these highways, caravansaries were erected" (—like those which can be noticed in the picture—) or "small buildings in which a number of runners were stationed."

59

The other great road of the Incas lay through the level country between the Andes and the ocean. It was constructed in a different manner as demanded by the nature of the ground, which was for the most part low, and much of it sandy. The causeway was raised on a high embankment of earth, and defended on either side by a parapet or wall of clay; and trees and odoriferous shrubs were planted along the margin, regaling the sense of the traveller with their perfumes, and refreshing him by their shades, so grateful under the burning sky of the tropics. In the strips of sandy waste, which occasionally intervened, where the light and volatile soil was incapable of sustaining a road, huge piles, many of them to be seen at this day, were driven into the ground to indicate the route to the traveller.

All along these highways, caravansaries, or *tambos,* as they were called, were erected, at the distance of ten or twelve miles from each other, for the accommodation, more particularly, of the Inca and his suite, and those who journeyed on the public business. There were few other travellers in Peru. Some of these buildings were on an extensive scale, consisting of a fortress, barracks, and other military works, surrounded by a parapet of stone, and covering a large tract of ground. These were evidently destined for the accommodation of the imperial armies, when on their march across the country. The care of the great roads was committed to the districts through which they passed, and a large number of hands was constantly employed under the Incas to keep them in repair. This was the more easily done in a country where the mode of travelling was altogether on foot; though the roads are said to have been so nicely constructed, that a carriage might have rolled over them as securely as on any of the great roads of Europe. Still, in a region where the elements of fire and water are both actively at work in the business of destruction, they must, without

constant supervision, have gradually gone to decay. Such has been their fate under the Spanish conquerors, who took no care to enforce the admirable system for their preservation adopted by the Incas. Yet the broken portions that still survive, here and there, like the fragments of the great Roman roads scattered over Europe, bear evidence to their primitive grandeur, and have drawn forth the eulogium from a discriminating traveller, usually not too profuse in his panegyric, that "the roads of the Incas were among the most useful and stupendous works ever executed by man".

The system of communication through their dominions was still further improved by the Peruvian sovereigns, by the introduction of posts, in the same manner as was done by the Aztecs. The Peruvian posts, however, established on all the great routes that conducted to the capital, were on a much more extended plan than those in Mexico. All along these routes, small buildings were erected, at the distance of less than five miles asunder, in each of which a number of runners, or *chasquis,* as they were called, were stationed to carry forward the despatches of government. These despatches were either verbal, or conveyed by means of *quipus,* and sometimes accompanied by a thread of the crimson fringe worn round the temples of the Inca, which was regarded with the same implicit deference as the signet ring of an Oriental despot.

The *chasquis* were dressed in a peculiar livery, intimating their profession. They were all trained to the employment, and selected for their speed and fidelity. As the distance each courier had to perform was small, and as he had ample time to refresh himself at the sta-

60

"... Runners, or chasquis, *as they were called, carried forward the despatches of government... The* Chasquis *were dressed in a peculiar livery, they were all trained to the employment and selected for their speed and fidelity" (opposite).*

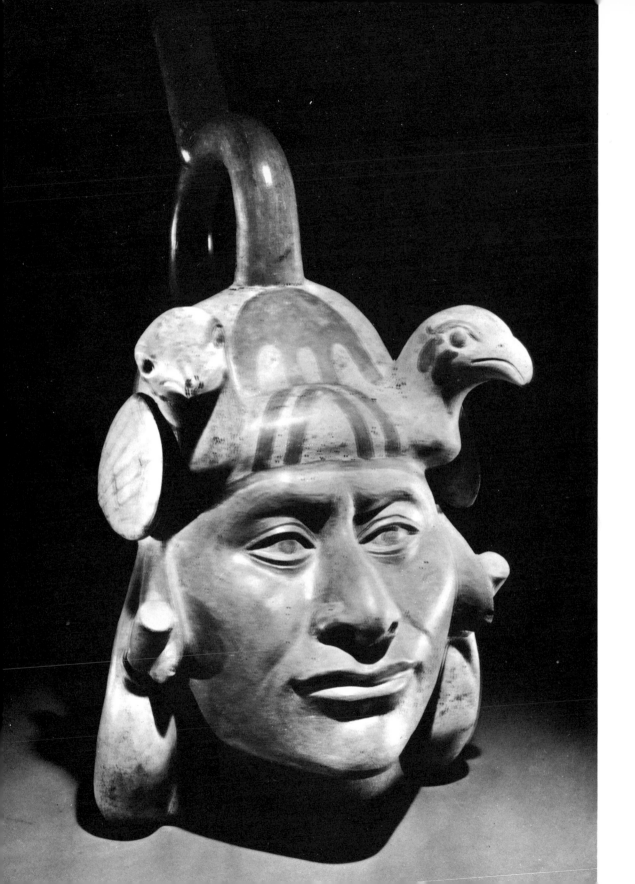

tions, they ran over the ground with great swiftness, and messages were carried through the whole extent of the long routes, at the rate of a hundred and fifty miles a day. The office of the *chasquis* was not limited to carrying despatches. They frequently brought various articles for the use of the Court; and in this way, fish from the distant ocean, fruits, game, and different commodities from the hot regions on the coast, were taken to the capital in good condition, and served fresh at the royal table. It is remarkable that this important institution should have been known to both the Mexicans and the Peruvians without any correspondence with one another; and that it should have been found among two barbarian nations of the New World, long before it was introduced among the civilized nations of Europe.

By these wise contrivances of the Incas, the most distant parts of the long-extended empire of Peru were brought into intimate relations with each other. And while the capitals of Christendom, but a few hundred miles apart, remained as far asunder as if seas had rolled between them, the great capitals Cuzco and Quito were placed by the high roads of the Incas in immediate correspondence. Intelligence from the numerous provinces was transmitted on the wings of the wind to the Peruvian metropolis, the great focus to which all the lines of communication converged. Not an insurrectionary movement could occur, not an invasion on the remotest frontier, before the tidings were conveyed to the capital, and the imperial armies were on their march across the magnificent roads of the country to suppress it. So admirable was the machinery contrived by the American despots for maintaining tranquillity throughout their dominions! It may remind us of the similar institutions of ancient Rome, when, under the Caesars, she was mistress of half the world.

A principal design of the great roads was to serve the purposes of military communication.

This very beautiful vase presents a warrior's head.

"The army was generally headed by the Inca in person". We can see here Huayna Capac carried to the battle.

It formed an important item of their military policy, which is quite as well worth studying as their municipal.

Notwithstanding the pacific professions of the Incas, and the pacific tendency, indeed, of their domestic institutions, they were constantly at war. It was by war that their paltry territory had been gradually enlarged to a powerful empire. When this was achieved, the capital, safe in its central position, was no longer shaken by these military movements, and the country enjoyed, in a great degree, the

63

blessings of tranquillity and order. But, however tranquil at heart, there is not reign upon record in which the nation was not engaged in war against the barbarous nations on the frontier. Religion furnished a plausible pretext for incessant aggression, and disguised the lust of conquest in the Incas, probably, from their own eyes, as well as from those of their subjects. Like the followers of Mahomet, bearing the sword in one hand and the Koran in the other, the Incas of Peru offered no alternative but the worship of the Sun or war.

It is true, their fanaticism—or their policy—showed itself in a milder form than was found in the descendants of the Prophet. Like the great luminary which they adored, they operated by gentleness more potent than violence. They sought to soften the hearts of the rude tribes around them, and melt them by acts of condescension and kindness. Far from provoking hostilities, they allowed time for the salutary example of their own institutions to work its effect, trusting that their less civilized neighbors would submit to their sceptre, from a conviction of the blessings it would secure to them. When this course failed, they employed other measures, but still of a pacific character; and endeavored by negotiation, by conciliatory treatment, and by presents to the leading men, to win them over to their dominion. In short, they practised all the arts familiar to the most subtle politician of a civilized land to secure the acquisition of empire. When all these expedients failed, they prepared for war.

Their levies were drawn from all the different provinces; though from some, where the character of the people was particulary hardy, more than from others. It seems probable that every Peruvian, who had reached a cerain age, might be called to bear arms. But the rotation of military service, and the regular drills, which took place twice or thrice in a month, of the inhabitants of every village, raised the soldiers generally above the rank of a raw militia. The Peruvian army, at first inconsiderable, came, with the increase of population, in the latter days of the empire to be very large, so that their monarchs could bring into the field, as contemporaries assure us, a force amounting to two hundred thousand men. They showed the same skill and respect for order in their military organization, as in other things. The troops were divided into bodies corresponding with our battalions and companies, led by officers, that rose, in regular gradation, from the lowest subaltern to the Inca noble, who was intrusted with the general command.

Their arms consisted of the usual weapons employed by nations, whether civilized or uncivilized, before the invention of powder, —bows and arrows, lances, darts, a short kind of sword, a battle-axe or partisan, and slings, with which they were very expert. Their spears and arrows were tipped with copper, or, more commonly, with bone, and the weapons of the Inca lords were frequently mounted with gold or silver. Their heads were protected by casques made either of wood or of the skins of wild animals, and sometimes richly decorated with metal and with precious stones, surmounted by the brilliant plumage of the tropical birds. These, of course, were the ornaments only of the higher orders. The great mass of the soldiery were dressed in the peculiar costume of their provinces, and their heads were wreathed with a sort of turban or roll of different-colored cloths, that produced a gay and animating effect. Their defensive armor consisted of a shield or buckler, and a close tunic of quilted cotton, in the same manner as with the Mexicans. Each company had its particular banner, and the imperial standard, high above all, displayed the glittering device and the rainbow,—the armorial ensign of the Incas, intimating their claims as children of the skies.

This is a very impressive statuette but it is only 10 inches high. (Paris, Musée de l'Homme).

By means of the thorough system of communication established in the country, a short time sufficed to draw the levies together from the most distant quarters. The army was put under the direction of some experienced chief, of the blood royal, or, more frequently, headed by the Inca in person. The march was rapidly performed, and with little fatigue to the soldier; for, all along the great routes, quarters were provided for him, at regular distances, where he could find ample accommodations. The country is still covered with the remains of military works, constructed of porphyry or granite, which tradition assures us were designed to lodge the Inca and his army.

At regular intervals, also, magazines were established, filled with grain, weapons, and the different munitions of war, with which the army was supplied on its march. It was the especial care of the government to see that these magazines, which were furnished from the stores of the Incas, were always well filled. When the Spaniards invaded the country, they supported their own armies for a long time on the provisions found in them. The Peruvian soldier was forbidden to commit any trespass on the property of the inhabitants whose territory lay in the line of march. Any violation of this order was punished with death. The soldier was clothed and fed by the industry of the people, and the Incas rightly resolved that he should not repay this by violence. Far from being a tax on the labors of the husband-man, or even a burden on his hospitality, the imperial armies traversed the country, from one extremity to the other, with as little inconvenience to the inhabitants, as would be created by a procession of peaceful burghers, or a muster of holiday soldiers for a review.

From the moment war was proclaimed, the Peruvian monarch used all possible expedition in assembling his forces, that he might antici-pate the movements of his enemies, and prevent a combination with their allies. It was, however, from the neglect of such a prin-ciple of combination, that the several nations of the country, who might have prevailed by confederated strength, fell one after another under the imperial yoke. Yet once in the field the Inca did not usually show any disposition to push his advantages to the utmost, and urge his foe to extremity. In every stage of the war, he was open to propositions for peace; and although he sought to reduce his enemies by

"Those sanguinary pages which cannot be pondered without a shudder..."—An officer presents the Inca Yupanqui with the head of an enemy chief (left). —"Religion furnished a plausible pretext for incessant agression": all should worship the Sun, like the subjects represented in the picture above.

carrying off their harvests and distressing them by famine, he allowed his troops to commit no unnecessary outrage on person or property. "We must spare our enemies", one of the Peruvian princes is quoted as saying, "or it will be our loss, since they and all that belong to them must soon be ours". It was a wise maxim, and, like most other wise maxims, founded equally on benevolence and prudence. The Incas adopted the policy claimed for the Romans by their countryman, who tells us that they gained more by clemency to the vanquished than by their victories.

In the same considerate spirit, they were most careful to provide for the security and comfort of their own troops; and, when a war was long protracted, or the climate proved unhealthy, they took care to relieve their men by frequent reinforcements, allowing the earlier recruits to return to their homes. But while thus economical of life, both in their own followers and in the enemy, they did not shrink from sterner measures when provoked by the ferocious or obstinate character of the resistance; and the Peruvian annals contain more than one of those sanguinary pages which cannot be pondered at the present day without a shudder. It should be added, that the beneficent policy, which I have been delineating as characteristic of the Incas, did not belong to all; and that there was more than one of the royal line who displayed a full measure of the bold and unscrupulous spirit of the conqueror.

The first step of the government, after the reduction of a country, was to introduce there the worship of the Sun. Temples were erected, and placed under the care of a numerous priesthood, who expounded to the conquered people the mysteries of their new faith, and dazzled them by the display of its rich and stately ceremonial. Yet the religion of the conquered was not treated with dishonor. The Sun was to be worshipped above all; but the images of their gods were removed to Cuzco and established in one the temples, to hold their rank among the inferior deities of the Peruvian Pantheon. Here they remained as hostages, in some sort, for the conquered nation, which would be the less inclined to forsake its allegiance, when by doing so it must leave its own gods in the hands of its enemies.

The Incas provided for the settlement of their new conquests, by ordering a census to be taken of the population, and a careful survey to be made of the country, ascertaining its products, and the character and capacity of its soil. A division of the territory was then made on the same principle with that adopted throughout their own kingdom; and their respective portions were assigned to the Sun, the sovereign, and the people. The amount of the last was regulated by the amount of the population, but the share of each individual was uniformly the same. It may seem strange, that any people should patiently have acquiesced in an arrangement which involved such a total surrender of property. But it was a conquered nation that did so, held in awe, on the least suspicion of meditating resistance, by armed garrisons, who were established at various commanding points throughout the country. It is probable, too, that the Incas made no greater changes than was essential to the new arrangement, and that they assigned estates, as far as possible, to their former proprietors. The curacas, in particular, were confirmed in their ancient authority; or, when it was found expedient to depose the existing curaca, his rightful heir was allowed to succeed him. Every respect was shown to the ancient usages and laws of the land, as far as was compatible with the fundamental institutions of the Incas. It must also be remembered, that the conquered tribes were, many of them, too little advanced in civilization to possess that attachment to the soil which belongs to a cultivated nation. But, to whatever it be referred, it seems probable that the extraor-

Ceremonial knife, with mythological figure. It is entirely made of gold and adorned with precious stones. (Private collection, photo by Giraudon).

dinary institutions of the Incas were established with little opposition in the conquered territories.

Yet the Peruvian sovereigns did not trust altogether to this show of obedience in their new vassals; and, to secure it more effectually, they adopted some expedients too remarkable to be passed by in silence.—Immediately after a recent conquest, the curacas and their families were removed for a time to Cuzco. Here they learned the language of the capital, became familiar with the manners and usages of the court, as well as with the general policy of government, and experienced such marks of favor from the sovereign as would be most grateful to their feelings, and might attach them most warmly to his person. Under the influence of these sentiments, they were again sent to rule over their vassals but still leaving their eldest sons in the capital, to remain there as a guaranty for their own fidelity, as well as to grace the court of the Inca.

Another expedient was of a bolder and more original character. This was nothing less than to revolutionize the language of the country. South America, like North, was broken up into a great variety of dialects, or rather languages, having little affinity with one another. This circumstance occasioned great embarrassment to the government in the administration of the different provinces, with whose idioms they were unacquainted. It was determined, therefore, to substitute one universal language, the *Quichua,*—the language of the court, the capital, and the surrounding country,—the richest and most comprehensive of the South American dialects. Teachers were provided in the towns and villages throughout the land, who were to give instruction to all, even the humblest classes; and it was intimated at the same time, that no one should be raised to any office of dignity or profit, who was unacquainted with this tongue. The curacas and other chiefs, who attended

On the steps of the great fortress at Cuzco, is this young flute-player dreaming of his ancestors' grandeur?

at the capital, became familiar with this dialect in their intercourse with the Court, and, on their return home, set the example of conversing in it among themselves. This example was imitated by their followers, and the Quichua gradually became the language of elegance and fashion, in the same manner as the Norman French was affected by all those who aspired to any consideration in England, after the Conquest. By this means, while each province retained its peculiar tongue, a beautiful medium of communication was introduced, which enabled the inhabitants of one part of the country to hold intercourse with every other, and the Inca and his deputies to communicate with all. This was the state of things on the arrival of the Spaniards. It must be admitted, that history furnishes few examples of more absolute authority than such a revolution in the language of an empire, at the bidding of a master.

Yet little less remarkable was another device of the Incas for securing the loyalty of their subjects. When any portion of the recent conquests showed a pertinacious spirit of disaffection, it was not uncommon to cause a part of the population, amounting, it might be, to ten thousand inhabitants or more, to remove to a distant quarter of the kingdom, occupied by ancient vassals of undoubted fidelity to the crown. A like number of these last was transplanted to the territory left vacant by the emigrants. By this exchange, the population was composed of two distinct races, who regarded each other with an eye of jealousy, that served as an effectual check on any mutinous proceeding. In time, the influence of the well-affected prevailed, supported, as they were, by royal authority, and by the silent working of the national institutions, to which the strange races became gradually accustomed. A spirit of loyalty sprang up by degrees in their bosoms, and, before a generation had passed away, the different tribes mingled in harmony together as members of the same community. Yet the different races continued to be distinguished by difference of dress; since, by the law of the land, every citizen was required to wear the costume of his native province. Neither could the colonist, who had been thus unceremoniously transplanted, return to his native district for, by another law, it was forbidden to any one to change his residence without license. He was settled for life. The Peruvian government ascribed to every man his local habitation, his sphere of action, nay, the very nature and quality of that action. He ceased to be a free agent; it might be almost said, that it relieved him of personal responsibility.

In following out this singular arrangement, the Incas showed as much regard for the comfort and convenience of the colonist as was compatible with the execution of their design. They were careful that the *mitimaes*, as these emigrants were styled, should be removed to climates most congenial with their own. The inhabitants of the cold countries were not transplanted to the warm, nor the inhabitants of the warm countries to the cold. Even their habitual occupations were consulted, and the fisherman was settled in the neighborhood of the ocean, or the great lakes; while such lands were assigned to the husbandman as were best adapted to the culture with which he was most familiar. And, as migration by many, perhaps by most, would be regarded as a calamity, the government was careful to show particular marks of favor to the *mitimaes*, and, by various privileges and immunities, to ameliorate their condition, and thus to reconcile them, if possible, to their lot.

The Peruvian institutions, though they may have been modified and matured under successive sovereigns, all bear the stamp of the same original,—were all cast in the same mould. The empire, strengthening and enlargkono yauento del ynga llama

The victorious monarch coming back to his capital. "The Inca, borne aloft in his golden chair, moved in solemn procession to the great temple of the Sun."

ing at every successive epoch of its history, was in its latter days, but the development, on a great scale, of what it was in miniature at its commencement, as the infant germ is said to contain within itself all the ramifications of the future monarch of the forest. Each succeeding Inca seemed desirous only to tread in the path, and carry out the plans, of his predecessor. Great enterprises, commenced under one, were continued by another, and completed by a third. Thus, while all acted on a regular plan, without any of the eccentric or retrograde movements which betray the agency of different individuals, the state seemed to be under the direction of a single hand, and steadily pursued, as if through one long reign, its great career of civilization and of conquest.

The ultimate aim of its institutions was domestic quiet. But it seemed as if this were to be obtained only by foreign war. Tranquillity in the heart of the monarchy, and war on its borders, was the condition of Peru. By this war it gave occupation to a part of its people, and, by the reduction and civilization of its barbarous neighbors, gave security to all. Every Inca sovereign, however mild and benevolent in his domestic rule, was a warrior, and led his armies in person. Each successive reign extended still wider the boundaries of the empire. Year after year saw the victorious monarch return laden with spoils, and followed by a throng of tributary chieftains to his capital. His reception there was a Roman triumph.

73

The whole of its numerous population poured out to welcome him, dressed in the gay and picturesque costumes of the different provinces, with banners waving above their heads, and strewing branches and flowers along the path of the conqueror. The Inca, borne aloft in his golden chair on the shoulders of his nobles, moved in solemn procession, under the triumphal arches that were thrown across the way, to the great temple of the Sun. There, without attendants,—for all but the monarch were excluded from the hallowed precincts,—the victorious prince, stripped of his royal insignia, barefooted, and with all humility, approached the awful shrine, and offered up sacrifice and thanksgiving to the glorious Deity who presided over the fortunes of the Incas. This ceremony concluded, the whole population gave itself up to festivity; music, revelry, and dancing were heard in every quarter of the capital, and illuminations and bonfires commemorated the victorious campaign of the Inca, and the accession of a new territory to his empire.

In this celebration we see much of the character of a religious festival. Indeed, the character of religion was impressed on all the Peruvian wars. The life of an Inca was one long crusade against the infidel, to spread wide the worship of the Sun, to reclaim the benighted nations from their brutish superstitions, and impart to them the blessings of a well-regulated government. This, in the favorite phrase of our day, was the "mission" of the Inca. It was also the mission of the Christian conqueror who invaded the empire of this same Indian potentate. Which of the two executed his mission most faithfully, history must decide.

Yet the Peruvian monarchs did not show a childish impatience in the acquisition of empire. They paused after a campaign, and allowed time for the settlement of one conquest before they undertook another; and, in this interval, occupied themselves with the quiet administration of their kingdom, and with the long progresses, which brought them into nearer intercourse with their people. During this interval, also, their new vassals had begun to accommodate themselves to the strange institutions of their masters. They learned to appreciate the value of a government which raised them above the physical evils of a state of barbarism, secured them protection of person, and a full participation in all the privileges enjoyed by their conquerors; and, as they became more familiar with the peculiar institutions of the country, habit, that second nature, attached them the more strongly to these institutions, from their very peculiarity. Thus, by degrees, and without violence, arose the great fabric of the Peruvian empire, composed of numerous independent and even hostile tribes, yet, under the influence of a common religion, common language, and common government, knit together as one nation, animated by a spirit of love for its institutions and devoted loyalty to its sovereign. What a contrast to the condition of the Aztec monarchy, on the neighboring continent, which, composed of the like heterogeneous materials, without any internal principle of cohesion, was only held together by the stern pressure, from without, of physical force!—Why the Peruvian monarchy should have fared no better than its rival, in its conflict with European civilization, will appear in the following pages.

3 - Peruvian religion - Deities - Gorgeous Temples - Festivals - Virgins of the Sun - Marriage.

It is a remarkable fact, that many, if not most, of the rude tribes inhabiting the vast American continent, however disfigured their creeds may have been in other respects by a childish superstition, had attained to the sublime conception of one Great Spirit, the Creator of the Universe, who, immaterial in his own nature, was not to be dishonored by an attempt at visible representation, and who, pervading all space, was not to be circumscribed within the walls of a temple. Yet these elevated ideas, so far beyond the ordinary range of the untutored intellect, do not seem to have led to the practical consequences that might have been expected; and few of the American nations have shown much solicitude for the maintenance of a religious worship, or found in their faith a powerful spring of action.

But, with progress in civilization, ideas more akin to those of civilized communities were gradually unfolded; a liberal provision was made, and a separate order instituted, for the services of religion, which were conducted with a minute and magnificent ceremonial, that challenged comparison, in some respects, with that of the most polished nations of Christendom. This was the case with the nations inhabiting the table-land of North America, and with the natives of Bogotá, Quito, Peru, and the other elevated regions on the great Southern continent. It was, above all, the case with the Peruvians, who claimed a divine original for the founders of their empire, whose laws all rested on a divine sanction, and whose domestic institutions and foreign wars were alike directed to preserve and propagate their faith. Religion was the basis of their polity, the very condition, as it were, of their social existence. The government of the Incas, in its essential principles, was a theocracy.

Yet, though religion entered so largely into the fabric and conduct of the political institutions of the people, their mythology, that is, the traditionary legends by which they affected to unfold the mysteries of the universe, was exceedingly mean and puerile. Scarce one of their traditions—except the beautiful one respecting the founders of their royal dynasty —is worthy of note, or throws much light on their own antiquities, or the primitive history

Is this face that of a priest? The head-dress is a mitre. (Museum of Lima).

Wall of a temple at Machu Picchu.

of man. Among the traditions of importance is one of the deluge, which they held in common with so many of the nations in all parts of the globe, and which they related with some particulars that bear resemblance to a Mexican legend.

Their ideas in respect to a future state of being deserve more attention. They admitted the existence of a soul hereafter, and connected with this a belief in the resurrection of the body. They assigned two distinct places for the residence of the good and of the wicked, the latter of which they fixed in the centre of the earth. The good they supposed were to pass a luxurious life of tranquillity and ease, which comprehended their highest notions of happiness. The wicked were to expiate their crimes by ages of wearisome labor. They associated with these ideas a belief in an evil principle or spirit, bearing the name of Cupay, whom they did not attempt to propitiate by sacrifices, and who seems to have been only a shadowy personification of sin, that exercised little influence over their conduct.

It was this belief in the resurrection of the body, which led them to preserve the body with so much solicitude, by a simple process, however, that, unlike the elaborate embalming of the Egyptians, consisted in exposing it to the action of the cold, exceedingly dry, and highly rarefied atmosphere of the mountains. As they believed that the occupations in the future world would have great resemblance to those of the present, they buried with the deceased noble some of his apparel, his utensils, and, frequently, his treasures; and completed the gloomy ceremony by sacrificing his wives and favorite domestics, to bear him company and do him service in the happy regions beyond the clouds. Vast mounds of an irregular, or, more frequently, oblong shape, penetrated by galleries running at right angles to each other, were raised over the dead, whose dried bodies or mummies have been found in considerable numbers, sometimes erect, but more often in the sitting posture, common to the Indian tribes of both continents. Treasures of great value have also been occasionally drawn from these monumental deposits, and have stimulated speculators to repeated excavations with the hope of similar good-fortune. It was a lottery like that of searching after mines, but where the chances have proved still more against the adventurers.

The Peruvians, like so many other of the Indian races, acknowledged a Supreme Being, the Creator and Ruler of the Universe, whom they adored under the different names of Pachacamac and Viracocha. No temple was raised to this invisible Being, save one only in the valley which took its name from the deity himself, not far from the Spanish city of Lima. Even this temple had existed there before the country came under the sway of the Incas, and was the great resort of Indian pilgrims from remote parts of the land; a circumstance which suggests the idea, that the worship of this Great Spirit, though countenanced, perhaps, by their accommodating policy, did not originate with the Peruvian princes.

The deity whose worship they especially inculcated, and which they never failed to establish wherever their banners were known to penetrate, was the Sun. It was he, who, in a particular manner, presided over the destinies of man; gave light and warmth to the nations, and life to the vegetable world; whom they reverenced as the father of their royal dynasty, the founder of their empire; and whose temples rose in every city and almost every village throughout the land, while his altars smoked with burnt offerings,—a form of sacrifice peculiar to the Peruvians among the semi-civilized nations of the New World.

Besides the Sun, the Incas acknowledged various objects of worship in some way or other connected with this principal deity. Such was the Moon, his sister-wife; the Stars, revered as part of her heavenly train,—though the fairest of them, Venus, known to the Peruvians by the name of Chasca, or the "youth with the long and curling locks", was adored as the page of the Sun, whom he attends so closely in his rising and in his setting. They dedicated temples also to the Thunder and Lightning, in whom they recognized the Sun's dread ministers, and to the Rainbow, whom they worshipped as a beautiful emanation of their glorious deity.

In addition to these, the subjects of the Incas enrolled among their inferior deities many objects in nature, as the elements, the winds, the earth, the air, great mountains and rivers, which impressed them with ideas of sublimity and power, or were supposed in some way or other to exercise a mysterious influence over the destinies of man. They adopted also a notion, not unlike that professed by some of the schools of ancient philosophy, that every thing on earth had its archetype or idea, its *mother,* as they emphatically styled it, which they held sacred, as, in some sort, its spiritual essence. But their system, far from being limited even to these multiplied objects of devotion, embraced within its ample folds the numerous deities of the conquered nations, whose images were transported to the capital, where the burdensome charges of their worship were defrayed by their respective provinces. It was a rare stroke of policy in the Incas, who could thus accommodate their religion to their interests.

But the worship of the Sun constituted the peculiar care of the Incas, and was the object of their lavish expenditure. The most ancient of the many temples dedicated to this divinity was in the Island of Titicaca, whence the royal founders of the Peruvian line were said to have proceeded. From this circumstance, this sanctuary was held in peculiar veneration.

78

"The Peruvians acknowledged a Supreme Being, the Creator and Ruler of the Universe... (but they believed that) the Sun presided over the destinies of man".

Every thing which belonged to it, even the broad fields of maize, which surrounded the temple, and formed part of its domain, imbibed a portion of its sanctity. The yearly produce was distributed among the different public magazines, in small quantities to each, as something that would sanctify the remainder of the store. Happy was the man who could secure even an ear of the blessed harvest for his own granary!

But the most renowned of the Peruvian temples, the pride of the capital, and the wonder of the empire, was at Cuzco, where, under the munificence of successive sovereigns, it had become so enriched, that it received the name of *Coricancha,* or "the Place of Gold". It consisted of a principal building and several chapels and inferior edifices, covering a large extent of ground in the heart of the city, and completely encompassed by a wall, which, with the edifices, was all constructed of stone. The work was of the kind already described in the other public buildings of the country, and was so finely executed, that a Spaniard, who saw it in its glory, assures us, he could call to mind only two edifices in Spain, which, for their workmanship, were at all to be compared with it. Yet this substantial, and, in some respects, magnificent structure, was thatched with straw!

The interior of the temple was the most worthy of admiration. It was literally a mine of gold. On the western wall was emblazoned a representation of the deity, consisting of a human countenance, looking forth from amidst innumerable rays of light, which emanated from it in every direction, in the same manner as the sun is often personified with us. The figure was engraved on a massive plate of gold of enormous dimensions thickly powdered with emeralds and precious stones. It was so situated in front of the great eastern portal, that the rays of the morning sun fell directly upon it at its rising, lighting up the whole apartment with an effulgence that seemed more than natural, and which was reflected back from the golden ornaments with which the walls and ceiling were everywhere incrusted. Gold, in the figurative language of the people was "the tears wept by the sun", and every part of the interior of the temple glowed with burnished plates and studs of the precious metal. The cornices, which surrounded the walls of the sanctuary, were of the same costly material; and a broad belt or frieze of gold, let into the stone-work, encompassed the whole exterior of the edifice.

Adjoining the principal structure were several chapels of smaller dimensions. One of them was consecrated to the Moon, the deity held next in reverence, as the mother of the Incas. Her effigy was delineated in the same manner as that of the Sun, on a vast plate that nearly covered one side of the apartment. But this plate, as well as all the decorations of the building, was of silver, as suited to the pale, silvery light of the beautiful planet. There were three other chapels, one of which was dedicated to the host of Stars, who formed the bright court of the Sister of the Sun; another was consecrated to his dread ministers of vengeance, the Thunder and the Lightning; and a third, to the Rainbow, whose many-colored arch spanned the walls of the edifice with hues almost as radiant as its own. There were besides several other buildings, or insulated apartments, for the accommodation of the numerous priests who officiated in the services of the temple.

All the plate, the ornaments, the utensils of every description, appropriated to the uses of religion, were of gold or silver. Twelve immense vases of the latter metal stood on the floor of the great saloon, filled with grain of the Indian corn; the censers for the perfumes, the ewers which held the water for sacrifice, the pipes which conducted it through subterraneous channels into the buildings, the reservoirs that received it, even the agricultural implements used in the gardens of the temple, were all of the same rich materials. The gardens, like those described, belonging to the royal palaces, sparkled with flowers of gold and silver, and various imitations of the vegetable kingdom. Animals, also, were to be found there,—among which the llama, with its golden fleece, was most conspicuous,—executed in the same style, and with a degree of skill, which, in this instance, probably, did not surpass the excellence of the material.

If the reader sees in this fairy picture only the romantic coloring of some fabulous *El Dorado,* he must recall what has been said before in reference to the palaces of the Incas, and consider that these "Houses of the Sun", as they were styled, were the common reservoir into which flowed all the streams of public and private benefaction throughout the empire. Some of the statements, through credulity, and others, in the desire of exciting admiration, may be greatly exaggerated; but, in the coincidence of contemporary testimony, it is not easy to determine the exact line which should mark the measure of our skepticism. Certain it is, that the glowing picture I have given is warranted by those who saw these buildings in their pride, or shortly after they had been despoiled by the cupidity of their countrymen. Many of the costly articles were buried by the natives, or thrown into the waters of the rivers and the lakes; but enough remained to attest the unprecedented opulence of these religious establishments. Such things as were in their nature portable were speedily removed, to gratify the craving of the Conquerors, who even tore away the solid cornices and frieze of gold from the great temple, filling the vacant places with the cheaper, but —since it affords no temptation to avarice— more durable, material of plaster. Yet even thus shorn of their splendor, the venerable edifices still presented an attraction to the spoiler, who found in their dilapidated walls an inexhaustable quarry for the erection of other buildings. On the very ground once crowned by the gorgeous Coricancha rose the stately church of St. Dominic, one of the most magnificent structures of the New World. Fields of maize and lucerne now bloom on the spot which glowed with the golden gardens of the temple; and the friar chants his orisons within the consecrated precincts once occupied by the Children of the Sun.

Besides the great temple of the Sun, there was a large number of inferior temples and religious houses in the Peruvian capital and its environs, amounting, as is stated, to three or four hundred. For Cuzco was a sanctified spot, venerated not only as the abode of the Incas, but of all those deities who presided over the motley nations of the empire. It was the city beloved of the Sun; where his worship was maintained in its splendor; "where every fountain, pathway, and wall", says an ancient chronicler, "was regarded as a holy mystery". And unfortunate was the Indian noble who, at some period or other of his life, had not made his pilgrimage to the Peruvian Mecca.

Other temples and religious dwellings were scattered over the provinces; and some of them constructed on a scale of magnificence, that almost rivalled that of the metropolis. The attendants on these composed an army of themselves. The whole number of functionaries, including those of the sacerdotal order, who officiated at the Coricancha alone, was no less than four thousand.

At the head of all, both here and throughout the land, stood the great High-Priest, or Villac Vmu, as he was called. He was second only

"Perhaps the most magnificent of all the national solemnities was the feast of Raymi, held at the period of the summer solstice... On this occasion, the Indian nobles from the different quarters of the country thronged to the capital".—Notice, on this picture evoking the celebration of the Raymi, the presence of the Moon, also worshipped by the Incas: the Moon "sister-wife" of the Sun and the Stars were "revered as part of her heavenly train".

la gran pas cua
so lene del sol

to the Inca in dignity, and was usually chosen from his brothers or nearest kindred. He was appointed by the monarch, and held his office for life; and he, in turn, appointed to all the subordinate stations of his own order. This order was very numerous. Those members of it who officiated in the House of the Sun, in Cuzco, were taken exclusively from the sacred race of the Incas. The ministers in the provincial temples were drawn from the families of the curacas; but the office of high-priest in

This figure, judging from the source of the statuette, would come from the north of Peru.

each district was reserved for one of the blood royal. It was designed by this regulation to preserve the faith in its purity, and to guard against any departure from the stately ceremonial which it punctiliously prescribed.

The sacerdotal order, though numerous, was not distinguished by any peculiar badge or costume from the rest of the nation. Neither was it the sole depository of the scanty science of the country, nor was it charged with the business of instruction, nor with those parochial duties, if they may so be called, which bring the priest in contact with the great body of the people,—as was the case in Mexico. The cause of this peculiarity may probably be traced to the existence of a superior order, like that of the Inca nobles, whose sanctity of birth so far transcended all human appointments, that they in a manner engrossed whatever there was of religious veneration in the people. They were, in fact, the holy order of the state. Doubtless, any of them might, as very many of them did, take on themselves the sacerdotal functions; and their own insignia and peculiar privileges were too well understood to require any further badge to separate them from the people.

The duties of the priest were confined to ministration in the temple. Even here his attendance was not constant, as he was relieved after a stated interval by other brethren of his order, who succeeded one another in regular rotation. His science was limited to an acquaintance with the fasts and festivals of his religion, and the appropriate ceremonies which distinguished them. This, however frivolous might be its character, was no easy acquisition; for the ritual of the Incas involved a routine of observances, as complex and elaborate as ever distinguished that of any nation, whether pagan or Christian. Each month had its appropriate festival, or rather festivals. The four principal had reference to the Sun, and commemorated the great periods of his annual progress, the solstices and equinoxes. Perhaps the most magnificent of all the national solemnities was the feast of Raymi, held at the period of the summer solstice, when the Sun, having touched the southern extremity of his course, retraced his path, as if to gladden the hearts of his chosen people by his presence. On this occasion, the Indian nobles from the different quarters of the country thronged to the capital to take part in the great religious celebration.

Those stairs, hewn in the rock, lead to a temple of Machu Picchu.

For three days previous, there was a general fast, and no fire was allowed to be lighted in the dwellings. When the appointed day arrived, the Inca and his court, followed by the whole population of the city, assembled at early dawn in the great square to greet the rising of the Sun. They were dressed in their gayest apparel, and the Indian lords vied with each other in the display of costly ornaments and jewels on their persons, while canopies of gaudy feather-work and richly tinted stuffs, borne by the attendants over their heads, gave to the great square, and the streets that emptied into it, the appearance of being spread over with one vast and magnificent awning. Eagerly they watched the coming of their deity, and, no sooner did his first yellow rays strike the turrets and loftiest buildings of the capital, than a shout of gratulation broke forth from the assembled multitude, accompanied by songs of triumph, and the wild melody of barbaric instruments, that swelled louder and louder as his bright orb, rising above the mountain range towards the east, shone in full splendor on his votaries. After the usual ceremonies of adoration, a libation was offered to the great deity by the Inca, from a huge golden vase, filled with the fermented liquor of maize or of maguey, which, after the monarch had tasted it himself, he dispensed among his royal kindred. These ceremonies completed, the vast assembly was arranged in order of procession, and took its way towards the Coricancha.

As they entered the street of the sacred edifice, all divested themselves of their sandals, except the Inca and his family, who did the same on passing through the portals of the temple, where none but these august personages were admitted. After a decent time spent in devotion, the sovereign, attended by his courtly train, again appeared, and preparations were made to commence the sacrifice. This, with the Peruvians, consisted of animals, grain, flowers, and sweet-scented gums; sometimes of human beings, on which occasions a child or beautiful maiden was usually selected as the victim. But such sacrifices were rare, being reserved to celebrate some great public event, as a coronation, the birth of a royal heir, or a great victory. They were never followed by those cannibal repasts familiar to the Mexicans, and to many of the fierce tribes conquered by the Incas. Indeed, the conquests of these princes might well be deemed a blessing to the Indian nations, if it were only from their suppression of cannibalism, and the diminution, under their rule, of human sacrifices.

At the feast of Raymi, the sacrifice usually offered was that of the llama; and the priest, after opening the body of his victim, sought in the appearances which it exhibited to read the lesson of the mysterious future. If the auguries were unpropitious, a second victim was slaughtered, in the hope of receiving some more comfortable assurance. The Peruvian augur might have learned a good lesson of the Roman,—to consider every omen as favorable, which served the interests of his country.

A fire was then kindled by means of a concave mirror of polished metal, which, collecting the rays of the sun into a focus upon a quantity of dried cotton, speedily set it on fire. It was the expedient used on the like occasions in ancient Rome, at least under the reign of the pious Numa. When the sky was overcast, and the face of the good deity was hidden from his worshippers, which was esteemed a bad omen, fire was obtained by means of friction. The sacred flame was intrusted to the care of the Virgins of the Sun, and if, by any neglect, it was suffered to go out in the course of the year, the event was regarded as a calamity that boded some strange disaster to the monarchy. A burnt offering of the victims was then made on the altars of the deity. This sacrifice was but the prelude to the slaughter of a great number of llamas, part of the flocks of the Sun, which furnished a banquet not only for the Inca and his Court, but for the people, who made amends at these festivals for the frugal fare to which they were usually condemned. A fine bread or cake, kneaded of maize flour by the fair hands

Left: this musician whose picture was taken nowadays in Peru seems to be a survival of

times past. Below: music instruments in terra cotta from the Inca period, kept in the Museum of Lima.

"Dancing and drinking were the favorite pastimes of the Peruvians..." On the picture above, a dancer accompanied by a very lightly dressed woman.

of the Virgins of the Sun, was also placed on the royal board, where the Inca, presiding over the feast, pledged his great nobles in generous goblets of the fermented liquor of the country, and the long revelry of the day was closed at night by music and dancing. Dancing and drinking were the favorite pastimes of the Peruvians. These amusements continued for several days, though the sacrifices terminated on the first.—Such was the great festival of Raymi; and the recurrence of this and similar festivities gave relief to the monotonous routine of toil prescribed to the lower orders of the community.

In the distribution of bread and wine at this high festival, the orthodox Spaniards, who first came into the country, saw a striking resemblance to the Christian communion; as in the practice of confession and penance, which, in a most irregular form, indeed, seems to have been used by the Peruvians, they discerned a coincidence with another of the sacraments of the Church. The good fathers were fond of tracing such coincidences, which they considered as the contrivance of Satan, who thus endeavored to delude his victims by counterfeiting the blessed rites of Christianity. Others, in a different vein, imagined that they saw in such analogies the evidence, that some of the primitive teachers of the Gospel, perhaps an apostle himself, had paid a visit to these distant regions, and scattered over them the seeds of religious truth. But it seems hardly necessary to invoke the Prince of Darkness, or the intervention of the blessed saints, to account for coincidences which have existed in countries far removed from the light of Christianity, and in ages, indeed, when its light had not yet risen on the world. It is much more reasonable to refer such casual points of resemblance to the general constitution of man, and the necessities of his moral nature.

Another singular analogy with Roman

Very old vase evoking a very unhappy man : he is crying.

86

Catholic institutions is presented by the Virgins of the Sun, the "elect", as they were called, to whom I have already had occasion to refer. These were young maidens, dedicated to the service of the deity, who, at a tender age, were taken from their homes, and introduced into convents, where they were placed under the care of certain elderly matrons, *mamaconas,* who had grown grey within their walls. Under these venerable guides, the holy virgins were instructed in the nature of their religious duties. They were employed in spinning and embroidery, and, with the fine hair of the vicuña, wove the hangings for the temples, and the apparel for the Inca and his household. It was their duty, above all, to watch over the sacred fire obtained at the festival of Raymi. From the moment they entered the establishment, they were cut off from all connection with the world, even with their own family and friends. No one but the Inca, and the Coya or queen, might enter the consecrated precincts. The greatest attention was paid to their morals, and visitors were sent every year to inspect the institutions, and to report on the state of their discipline. Woe to the unhappy maiden who was detected in an intrigue! By the stern law of the Incas, she was to be buried alive, her lover was to be strangled, and the town or village to which he belonged was to be razed to the ground, and "sowed with stones", as if to efface every memorial of his existence. One is astonished to find so close a resemblance between the institutions of the American Indian, the ancient Roman, and the modern Catholic! Chastity and purity of life are virtues in woman, that would seem to be of equal estimation with the barbarian and with the civilized.—Yet the ultimate destination of the inmates of these religious houses was materially different.

The great establishment at Cuzco consisted wholly of maidens of the royal blood, who amounted, it is said, to no less than fifteen

The art of textile was carried very far under the Incas.

89

hundred. The provincial convents were supplied from the daughters of the curacas and inferior nobles, and, occasionally, where a girl was recommended by great personal attractions, from the lower classes of the people. The "Houses of the Virgins of the Sun' consisted of low ranges of stone buildings, covering a large extent of ground, surrounded by high walls, which excluded those within entirely from observation. They were provided with every accommodation for the fair inmates, and were embellished in the same sumptuous and costly manner as the palaces of the Incas, and the temples; for they received the particular care of government, as an important part of the religious establishment.

Yet the career of all the inhabitants of these cloisters was not confined within their narrow walls. Though Virgins of the Sun, they were brides of the Inca, and, at a marriageable age, the most beautiful among them were selected for the honors of his bed, and transferred to the royal seraglio. The full complement of this amounted in time not only to hundreds, but thousands, who all found accommodations in his different palaces throughout the country. When the monarch was disposed to lessen the number of his establishment, the concubine

Reconstitution of a girls' educational establishment at Pachacamac.

with whose society he was willing to dispense returned, not to her former monastic residence, but to her own home; where, however humble might be her original condition, she was maintained in great state.

The great nobles of Peru were allowed, like their sovereign, a plurality of wives. The people, generally, whether by law, or by necessity stronger than law, were more happily limited to one. Marriage was conducted in a manner that gave it quite as original a character as belonged to the other institutions of the country. On an appointed day of the year, all those of a marriageable age—which, having reference to their ability to take charge of a family, in the males was fixed at not less than twenty-four years, and in the women at eighteen or twenty—were called together in the great squares of their respective towns and villages, throughout the empire. The Inca presided in person over the assembly of his own kindred, and taking the hands of the different couples who were to be united, he placed them within each other, declaring the parties man and wife. The same was done by the curacas towards all persons of their own or inferior degree in their several districts. This was the simple form of marriage in Peru.

"A singular analogy with Roman Catholic institutions is presented by the Virgins of the Sun... They were employed in spinning and embroidery."

No one was allowed to select a wife beyond the community to which he belonged. Nor was any but the sovereign authorized to dispense with the law of nature—or at least, the usual law of nations—so far as to marry his own sister. No marriage was esteemed valid without the consent of the parents; and the preference of the parties, it is said, was also to be consulted; though, considering the barriers imposed by the prescribed age of the candidates, this must have been within rather narrow and whimsical limits. A dwelling was got ready for the new-married pair at the charge of the district, and the prescribed portion of land assigned for their maintenance. —The simple ceremony of marriage was followed by general festivities among the friends of the parties, which lasted several days; and as every wedding took place on the same day, and as there were few families who had not someone of their members or their kindred personally interested, there was one universal bridal jubilee throughout the empire.

The extraordinary regulations respecting marriage under the Incas are eminently characteristic of the genius of the government; which, far from limiting itself to matters of public concern, penetrated into the most private recesses of domestic life. No Peruvian was too low for the fostering vigilance of government. None was so high that he was not made to feel his dependence upon it in every act of his life. His very existence as an individual was absorbed in that of the community. His hopes and his fears, his joys and his sorrows, the tenderest sympathies of his nature, were all to be regulated by law. He was not allowed even to be happy in his own way. The government of the Incas was the mildest, —but the most searching of despotisms.

"Marriage was conducted in a manner that gave it quite as original a character as belonged to the other institutions of the country... A dwelling was got ready for the new-married pair at the charge of the district".

4 - Education - Quipus - Astronomy - Agriculture - Aqueducts - Guano - Important esculents.

"Science was not intended for the people; but for those of generous blood. Persons of low degree are only puffed up by it, and rendered vain and arrogant. Neither should such meddle with the affairs of government; for this would bring high offices into disrepute, and cause detriment to the state". Such was the favorite maxim, often repeated, of Tupac Inca Yupanqui, one of the most renowned of the Peruvian sovereigns. It may seem strange that such a maxim should ever have been proclaimed in the New World, where popular institutions have been established on a more extensive scale than was ever before witnessed; where government rests wholly on the people; and education—at least, in the great northern division of the continent—is mainly directed to qualify the people for the duties of government. Yet this maxim was strictly conformable to the genius of the Peruvian monarchy, and may serve as a key to its habitual policy; since, while it watched with unwearied solicitude over its subjects, provided for their physical necessities, was mindful of their morals, and showed, throughout, the affectionate concern of a parent for his children, it yet regarded them only as children, who were never to emerge from the state of pupilage, to act or to think for themselves, but whose whole duty was comprehended in the obligation of implicit obedience.

Such was the humiliating condition of the people under the Incas while the numerous families of the blood royal enjoyed the benefit of all the light of education, which the civilization of the country could afford; and, long after the Conquest, the spots continued to be pointed out where the seminaries had existed for their instruction. These were placed under the care of the *amautas,* or "wise men", who engrossed the scanty stock of science—if science it could be called—possessed by the Peruvians, and who were the sole teachers of youth. It was natural that the monarch should take a lively interest in the instruction of the young nobility, his own kindred. Several of the Peruvian princes are said to have built their palaces in the neighborhood of the schools, in order that they might the more easily visit them and listen to the lectures of the amautas, which they occasionally reinforced by a homily of their own. In these schools, the royal pupils were instructed in all the different kinds of knowledge in which their teachers were versed, with especial reference to the stations they were to occupy in after-life. They studied the laws, and the principles of administering the government,

Tupac Inca Yupanqui: "Science was not intended for the people... persons of low degree are only puffed up by it, and rendered vain and arrogant".

93

in which many of them were to take part. They were initiated in the peculiar rites of their religion, most necessary to those who were to assume the sacerdotal functions. They learned also to emulate the achievements of their royal ancestors by listening to the chronicles compiled by the amautas. They were taught to speak their own dialect with purity and elegance; and they became acquainted with the mysterious science of the quipus, which supplied the Peruvians with the means of communicating their ideas to one another, and of transmitting them to future generations.

The quipu was a cord about two feet long, composed of different colored threads tightly twisted together, from which a quantity of smaller threads were suspended in the manner of a fringe. The threads were of different colors and were tied into knots. The word *quipu,* indeed, signifies *a knot.* The colors denoted sensible objects; as, for instance, *white* represented *silver,* and *yellow, gold.* They sometimes also stood for abstract ideas. Thus, *white* signified *peace,* and *red, war.* But the quipus were chiefly used for arithmetical purposes. The knots served instead of ciphers, and could be combined in such a manner as to represent numbers to any amount they required. By means of these they went through their calculations with great rapidity, and the Spaniards who first visited the country bear testimony to their accuracy.

Officers were established in each of the districts, who, under the title of *quipucamayus,* or "keepers of the quipus", were required to furnish the government with information on various important matters. One had charge of the revenues, reported the quantity of raw material distributed among the laborers, the quality and quantity of the fabrics made from it, and the amount of stores, of various kinds, paid into the royal magazines. Another exhibited the register of births and deaths,

the marriages, the number of those qualified to bear arms, and the like details in reference to the population of the kingdom. These returns were annually forwarded to the capital, where they were submitted to the inspection of officers acquainted with the art of deciphering these mystic records. The government was thus provided with a valuable mass of statistical information, and the skeins of many-colored threads, collected and carefully preserved, constituted what might be called the national archives.

But, although the quipus sufficed for all the purposes of arithmetical computation demanded by the Peruvians, they were incompetent so represent the manifold ideas and images which are expressed by writing. Even here, however, the invention was not

"The colors of the Quipus *denoted sensible objects;... the knots served instead of ciphers... officers were established in each of the districts, under the title of "keepers of the quipus".*

without its use. For, independently of the direct representation of simple objects, and even of abstract ideas, to a very limited extent, as above noticed, it afforded great help to the memory by way of association. The peculiar knot or color, in this way, suggested what it could not venture to represent; in the same manner—to borrow the homely illustration of an old writer—as the number of the Commandment calls to mind the Commandment itself. The quipus, thus used, might be regarded as the Peruvian system of mnemonics.

Annalists were appointed in each of the principal communities, whose business it was to record the most important events which occurred in them. Other functionaries of a higher character, usually the amautas, were intrusted with the history of the empire, and were selected to chronicle the great deeds of the reigning Inca, or of his ancestors. The narrative, thus concocted, could be communicated only by oral tradition; but the quipus served the chronicler to arrange the incidents with method, and to refresh his memory. The story, once treasured up in the mind, was indelibly impressed there by frequent repetition. It was repeated by the amauta to his pupils, and in this way history, conveyed partly by oral tradition, and partly by arbitrary signs, was handed down from generation to generation, with sufficient discrepancy of details, but with a general conformity of outline to the truth.

The Peruvian quipus were, doubtless, a wretched substitute for that beautiful contrivance, the alphabet, which, employing a few simple characters as the representatives of sounds, instead of ideas, is able to convey the most delicate shades of thought that ever passed through the mind of man. The Peruvian invention, indeed, was far below that of the hieroglyphics, even below the rude picture-writing of the Aztecs; for the latter art, however incompetent to convey abstract ideas, could depict sensible objects with tolerable accuracy. It is evidence of the total ignorance in which the two nations remained of each other, that the Peruvians should have borrowed nothing of the hieroglyphical system of the Mexicans, and this, notwithstanding that the existence of the maguey plant, *agave,* in South America might have furnished them with the very material used by the Aztecs for the construction of their maps.

It is impossible to contemplate without interest the struggles made by different nations, as they emerge from barbarism, to supply themselves with some visible symbols of thought,—that mysterious agency by which the mind of the individual may be put in communication with the minds of a whole community. The want of such a symbol is itself the greatest impediment to the progress of civilization. For what is it but to imprison the thought, which has the elements of immortality, within the bosom of its author, or of the small circle who come in contact with him, instead of sending it abroad to give light to thousands, and to generations yet unborn! Not only is such a symbol an essential element of civilization, but it may be assumed as the very criterion of civilization; for the intellectual advancement of a people will keep pace pretty nearly with its facilities for intellectual communication.

Yet we must be careful not to underrate the real value of the Peruvian system; nor to suppose that the quipus were as awkward an instrument, in the hand of a practised native, as they would be in ours. We know the effect of habit in all mechanical operations, and the

Spaniards bear constant testimony to the adroitness and accuracy of the Peruvians in this. Their skill is not more surprising than the facility with which habit enables us to master the contents of a printed page, comprehending thousands of separate characters, by a single glance, as it were, though each character must require a distinct recognition by the eye, and that, too, without breaking the chain of thought in the reader's mind. We must not hold the invention of the quipus too lightly, when we reflect that they supplied the means of calculation demanded for the affairs of a great nation, and that, however insufficient, they afforded no little help to what aspired to the credit of literary composition.

The office of recording the national annals was not wholly confined to the amautas. It was assumed in part by the *haravecs,* or poets, who selected the most brilliant incidents for their songs or ballads, which were chanted at the royal festivals and at the table of the Inca. In this manner, a body of traditional minstrelsy grew up, like the British and Spanish ballad poetry, by means of which the name of many a rude chieftain, that might have perished for want of a chronicler, has been borne down the tide of rustic melody to later generations.

Yet history may be thought not to gain much by this alliance with poetry; for the domain of the poet extends over an ideal realm peopled with the shadowy forms of fancy, that bear little resemblance to the rude realities of life. The Peruvian annals may be deemed to show somewhat of the effects of this union, since there is a tinge of the marvellous spread over them down to the very latest period, which, like a mist before the reader's eye, makes it difficult to distinguish between fact and fiction.

The poet found a convenient instrument for his purposes in the beautiful Quichua dialect. We have already seen the extraordinary measures taken by the Incas for propagating their language throughout their empire. Thus naturalized in the remotest provinces, it became enriched by a variety of exotic words and idioms, which, under the influence of the Court and of poetic culture, if I may so express myself, was gradually blended, like some finished mosaic made up of coarse and disjointed materials, into one harmonious whole. The Quichua became the most comprehensive and various, as well as the most elegant, of the South American dialects.

Besides the compositions already noticed, the Peruvians, it is said, showed some talent for theatrical exhibitions; not those barren pantomines which, addressed simply to the eye, have formed the amusement of more than one rude nation. The Peruvian pieces aspired to the rank of dramatic compositions, sustained by character and dialogue, founded sometimes on themes of tragic interest, and at others on such as, from their light and social character, belong to comedy. Of the execution of these pieces we have now no means of judging. It was probably rude enough, as befitted an unformed people. But, whatever may have been the execution, the mere conception of such an amusement is a proof of refinement that honorably distinguishes the Peruvian from the other American races, whose pastime was war, or the ferocious sports that reflect the image of it.

The intellectual character of the Peruvians, indeed, seems to have been marked rather by a tendency to refinement than by those hardier qualities which insure success in the severer walks of science. In these they were behind several of the semi-civilized nations of the New World. They had some acquaintance with geography, so far as related to their own empire, which was indeed extensive; and they constructed maps with lines raised on them to denote the boundaries and localities, on a similar principle with those formerly used by the blind. In astronomy, they appear to have made but moderate proficiency. They divided the year into twelve lunar months, each of which, having its own name, was distinguished by its appropriate festival. They had, also, weeks; but of what length, whether of seven, nine, or ten days, is uncertain. As their lunar year would necessarily fall short of the true time, they rectified their calendar by solar observations made by means of a number of cylindrical columns raised on the high lands round Cuzco, which served them for taking azimuths; and, by measuring their shadows, they ascertained the exact times of the solstices. The period of the equinoxes they determined by the help of a solitary pillar, or gnomon, placed in the centre of a circle, which was described in the area of the great temple, and traversed by a diameter that was drawn from east to west. When the shadows were scarcely visible under the noontide rays of the sun, they said that "the god sat with all his light upon the column". Quito, which lay immediately under the equator, where the vertical rays of the sun threw no shadow at noon, was held in especial veneration as the favored abode of the great deity. The period of the equinoxes was celebrated by public rejoicings. The pillar was crowned by the golden chair of the Sun, and, both then and at the solstices, the columns were hung with garlands, and offerings of flowers and fruits were made, while high festival was kept throughout the empire. By these periods the Peruvians regulated their religious rites and ceremonial, and prescribed the nature of their agricultural labors. The year itself took its departure from the date of the winter solstice.

This meagre account embraces nearly all that has come down to us of Peruvian astronomy. It may seem strange that a nation, which had proceeded thus far in its observa-

tions, should have gone no farther; and that, notwithstanding its general advance in civilization, it should in this science have fallen so far short, not only of the Mexicans, but of the Muyscas, inhabiting the same elevated regions of the great southern plateau with themselves. These latter regulated their calendar on the same general plan of cycles and periodical series as the Aztecs, approaching yet nearer to the system pursued by the people of Asia.

It might have been expected that the Incas, the boasted children of the Sun, would have made a particular study of the phenomena of the heavens, and have constructed a calendar on principles as scientific as that of their semi-civilized neighbors. One historian, indeed, assures us that they threw their years into cycles of ten, a hundred, and a thousand years, and that by these cycles they regulated their chronology. But this assertion—not improbable in itself—rests on a writer but little gifted with the spirit of criticism, and is counter-balanced by the silence of every higher and earlier authority, as well as by the absence of any monument, like those found among other American nations, to attest the existence of such a calendar. The inferiority of the Peruvians may be, perhaps, in part explained by the fact of their priesthood being drawn exclusively from the body of the Incas, a privileged order of nobility, who had no need, by the assumption of superior learning, to fence themselves round from the approaches of the vulgar. The little true science possessed by the Aztec priest supplied him with a key to unlock the mysteries of the heavens, and the false system of astrology which he built upon it gave him credit as a being who had something of divinity in his own nature. But the Inca noble was divine by birth. The illusory study of astrology, so captivating to the unenlightened mind, engaged no share of his attention. The only persons in Peru,

"The only persons in Peru, who claimed the power of reading the mysterious future, were the diviners, who combined with their pretensions some skill in the healing art".

who claimed the power of reading the mysterious future, were the diviners, men who, combining with their pretensions some skill in the healing art, resembled the conjurors found among many of the Indian tribes. But the office was held in little repute, except among the lower classes, and was abandoned to those whose age and infirmity disqualified them for the real business of life.

The Peruvians had knowledge of one or two constellations, and watched the motions of the planet Venus, to which, as we have seen, they dedicated altars. But their ignorance of the first principles of astronomical science is shown by their ideas of eclipses, which, they supposed, denoted some great derangement of the planet; and when the moon labored under one of these mysterious infirmities, they sounded their instruments, and filled the air with shouts and lamentations, to rouse her from her lethargy. Such puerile conceits as these form a striking contrast with the real knowledge of the Mexicans, as displayed in their hieroglyphical maps, in which the true cause of this phenomenon is plainly depicted.

But, if less successful in exploring the heavens, the Incas must be admitted to have surpassed every other American race in their dominion over the earth. Husbandry was pursued by them on principles that may be truly called scientific. It was the basis of their political institutions. Having no foreign commerce, it was agriculture that furnished them with the means of their internal exchanges, their subsistence, and their revenues. We have seen their remarkable provisions for distributing the land in equal shares among the people, while they required every man, except the privileged orders, to assist in its cultivation. The Inca himself did not disdain to set the example. On one of the great annual festivals, he proceeded to the environs of Cuzco, attended by his Court, and, in the presence of all the people, turned up the earth with a golden plough,—or an instrument that served as such,—thus consecrating the occupation of the husbandman as one worthy to be followed by the Children of the Sun.

The patronage of the government did not stop with this cheap display of royal condescension, but was shown in the most efficient measures for facilitating the labors of the husbandman. Much of the country along the sea-coast suffered from want of water, as little or no rain fell there, and the few streams, in their short and hurried course from the mountains, exerted only a very limited influence on the wide extent of territory. The soil, it is true, was for the most part, sandy and sterile; but many places were capable of being reclaimed, and, indeed, needed only to be properly irrigated to be susceptible of extraordinary production. To these spots water was conveyed by means of canals and subterraneous aqueducts, executed on a noble scale. They consisted of large slabs of freestone nicely fitted together without cement, and discharged a volume of water sufficient, by means of latent ducts or sluices, to moisten the lands in the lower level, through which they passed. Some of these aqueducts were of great length. One that traversed the district of Condesuyu measured between four and five hundred miles. They were brought from some elevated lake or natural reservoir in the heart of the mountains, and were fed at intervals by other basins which lay in their route along the slopes of the sierra. In this descent, a passage was sometimes to be opened through rocks,—and this without the aid of iron tools; impracticable mountains were to be turned; rivers and marshes to be crossed; in short, the same obstacles were to be encountered as in the construction of their mighty roads. But the Peruvians seemed to take pleasure in wrestling with the difficulties of nature. Near Caxamarca, a tunnel is still

"... Canals and subterraneous aqueducts, executed on a noble scale, consisted of large slabs of freestone nicely fitted together without cement.

visible, which they excavated in the mountains, to give an outlet to the waters of a lake, when these rose to a height in the rainy season that threatened the country with inundation.

Most of these beneficent works of the Incas were suffered to go to decay by their Spanish conquerors. In some spots, the waters are still left to flow in their silent, subterraneous channels, whose windings and whose sources have been alike unexplored. Others, though partially dilapidated, and closed up with rubbish and the rank vegetation of the soil, still betray their course by occasional patches of fertility. Such are the remains in the valley of Nasca, a fruitful spot that lies between long tracts of desert; where the ancient water-courses of the Incas, measuring four or five feet in depth by three in width, and formed of large blocks of uncemented masonry, are conducted from an unknown distance.

The greatest care was taken that every occupant of the land through which these streams passed should enjoy the benefit of them. The quantity of water allotted to each was prescribed by law; and royal overseers superintended the distribution, and saw that it was faithfully applied to the irrigation of the ground.

The Peruvians showed a similar spirit of enterprise in their schemes for introducing cultivation into the mountainous parts of their domain. Many of the hills, though covered with a strong soil, were too precipitous to be tilled. These they cut into terraces, faced with rough stone, diminishing in regular gradation towards the summit; so that, while the lower strip, or *anden,* as it was called by the Spaniards, that belted round the base of the mountain, might comprehend hundreds of acres, the uppermost was only large enough to accommodate a few rows of Indian corn. Some of the eminences presented such a mass of solid rock, that, after being hewn into terraces, they were obliged to be covered deep

with earth, before they could serve the purpose of the husbandman. With such patient toil did the Peruvians combat the formidable obstacles presented by the face of their country! Without the use of the tools or the machinery familiar to the European, each individual could have done little; but acting in large masses, and under a common direction, they were enabled by indefatigable perseverance to achieve results, to have attempted which might have filled even the European with dismay.

In the same spirit of economical husbandry which redeemed the rocky sierra from the curse of sterility, they dug below the arid soil of the valleys, and sought for a stratum where some natural moisture might be found. These excavations, called by the Spaniards *hoyas,* or "pits", were made on a great scale, comprehending frequently more than an acre, sunk to the depth of fifteen or twenty feet, and fenced round within by a wall of *adobes,* or bricks baked in the sun. The bottom of the excavation, well prepared by a rich manure of the sardines,—a small fish obtained in vast quantities along the coast,—was planted with some kind of grain or vegetable.

The Peruvian farmers were well acquainted with the different kinds of manures, and made large use of them; a circumstance rare in the rich lands of the tropics, and probably not elsewhere practised by the rude tribes of America. They made great use of *guano,* the valuable deposit of sea-fowl, that has attracted so much attention, of late, from the agriculturists both of Europe and of our own country, and the stimulating and nutritious properties of which the Indians perfectly appreciated. This was found in such immense quantities on many of the little islands along the coast, as to have the appearance of lofty hills, which, covered with a white saline incrustation, led the Conquerors to give them the name of the *sierra nevada.*

100

The Incas took their usual precautions for securing the benefits of this important article to the husbandman. They assigned the small islands on the coast to the use of the respective districts which lay adjacent to them. When the island was large, it was distributed among several districts, and the boundaries for each were clearly defined. All encroachment on the rights of another was severely punished. And they secured the preservation of the fowl by penalties as stern as those by which the Norman tyrants of England protected their own game. No one was allowed to set foot on the island during the season for breeding, under pain of death; and to kill the birds at

"The Peruvians might be supposed to have had some knowledge of the plough... (in reality) the instrument which they used was a strong, sharp-pointed stake, traversed by a horizontal

piece, ten or twelve inches from the point, on which the ploughman might set his foot and force it into the ground... The women broke up the sods with their rakes".

any time was punished in the like manner.

With this advancement in agricultural science, the Peruvians might be supposed to have had some knowledge of the plough, in such general use among the primitive nations of the eastern continent. But they had neither the iron ploughshare of the Old World, nor had they animals for draught, which, indeed, were nowhere found in the New. The instrument which they used was a strong, sharp-pointed stake, traversed by a horizontal piece, ten or twelve inches from the point, on which the ploughman might set his foot and force it into the ground. Six or eight strong men were attached by ropes to the stake, and dragged it forcibly along,—pulling together, and keeping time as they moved by chanting their national songs, in which they were accompanied by the women who followed in their train, to break up the sods with their rakes. The mellow soil offered slight resistance; and the laborer, by long practice, acquired a dexterity which enabled him to turn up the ground to the requisite depth with astonishing facility. This substitute for the plough was but a clumsy contrivance; yet it is curious as the only specimen of the kind among the American aborigines, and was perhaps not much inferior to the wooden instrument introduced in its stead by the European conquerors.

It was frequently the policy of the Incas, after providing a deserted tract with the means for irrigation, and thus fitting it for the labors of the husbandman, to transplant there a colony of *mitimaes,* who brought it under cultivation by raising the crops best suited to the soil. While the peculiar character and capacity of the lands were thus consulted, a means of exchange of the different products was afforded to the neighboring provinces, which, from the formation of the country, varied much more than usual within the same limits. To facilitate these agricultural exchanges, fairs were instituted, which took place three times a month in some of the most populous places, where, as money was unknown, a rude kind of commerce was kept up by the barter of their respective products. These fairs afforded so many holidays for the relaxation of the industrious laborer.

Such were the expedients adopted by the Incas for the improvement of their territory; and, although imperfect, they must be allowed to show an acquaintance with the principles of agricultural science, that gives them some claim to the rank of a civilized people. Under their patient and discriminating culture, every inch of good soil was tasked to its greatest power of production; while the most unpromising spots were compelled to contribute something to the subsistence of the people.

Ropes and farming instruments on the wall of a country house. (Above).

Everywhere the land teemed with evidence of agricultural wealth, from the smiling valleys along the coast to the terraced steeps of the sierra, which, rising into pyramids of verdure, glowed with all the splendors of tropical vegetation.

The formation of the country was particularly favorable, as already remarked, to an infinite variety of products, not so much from its extent as from its various elevations, which, more remarkable, even, than those in Mexico, comprehend every degree of latitude from the equator to the polar regions. Yet, though the temperature changes in this region with the degree of elevation, it remains nearly the same in the same spots throughout the year; and the inhabitant feels none of those grateful vicissitudes of season which belong to the temperate latitudes of the globe. Thus, while the summer lies in full power on the burning regions of the palm and the cocoa-tree that fringe the borders of the ocean, the broad surface of the table-land blooms with the freshness of perpetual spring, and the higher summits of the Cordilleras are white with everlasting winter.

The Peruvians turned this fixed variety of climate, if I may so say, to the best account by cultivating the productions appropriate to each; and they particularly directed their attention to those which afforded the most nutriment to man. Thus, in the lower level were to be found the cassava-tree and the banana, that bountiful plant, which seems to have relieved man from the primeval curse—if it were not rather a blessing—of toiling for his sustenance. As the banana faded from the landscape, a good substitute was found in the maize, the great agricultural staple of both the northern and southern divisions of the American continent; and which, after its exportation to the Old World, spread so rapidly there, as to suggest the idea of its being indigenous to it. The Peruvians were well acquainted with the different modes of preparing this useful vegetable, though it seems they did not use it for bread, except at festivals; and they extracted a sort of honey from the stalk, and made an intoxicating liquor from the fermented grain, to which, like the Aztecs, they were immoderately addicted.

The temperate climate of the table-land furnished them with the maguey, *agave Americana,* many of the extraordinary qualities of which they comprehended, though not its most important one of affording a material for paper. Tobacco, too, was among the products of this elevated region. Yet the Peruvians differed from every other Indian nation to whom it was known, by using it only for medicinal purposes, in the form of snuff. They may have found a substitute for its narcotic qualities in the coca *(Erythroxylum Peruvianum),* or *cuca,* as called by the natives. This is a shrub which grows to the height of a man. The leaves when gathered are dried in the sun, and, being mixed with a little lime, form a preparation for chewing, much like the betel-leaf of the East. With a small supply of this cuca in his pouch, and a handful of roasted maize, the Peruvian Indian of our time performs his wearisome journeys, day after day, without fatigue, or, at least, without complaint. Even food the most invigorating is less grateful to him than his loved narcotic. Under the Incas, it is said to have been exclusively reserved for the noble orders. If so, the people gained one luxury by the Conquest; and, after that period, it was so extensively used by them, that this article constituted a

103

most important item of the colonial revenue of Spain. Yet, with the soothing charms of an opiate, this weed so much vaunted by the natives, when used to excess, is said to be attended with all the mischievous effects of habitual intoxication.

Higher up on the slopes of the Cordilleras, beyond the limits of the maize and of the *quinoa,*—a grain bearing some resemblance to rice, and largely cultivated by the Indians,— was to be found the potato, the introduction of which into Europe has made an era in the history of agriculture. Whether indigenous to Peru, or imported from the neighboring country of Chili, it formed the great staple of the more elevated plains, under the Incas, and its culture was continued to a height in the equatorial regions which reached many thousand feet above the limits of perpetual snow in the temperate latitudes of Europe. Wild specimens of the vegetable might be seen still higher, springing up spontaneously amidst the stunted shrubs that clothed the lofty sides of the Cordilleras, till these gradually subsided into the mosses and the short yellow grass, *pajonal,* which, like a golden carpet, was unrolled around the base of the mighty cones, that rose far into the regions of eternal silence, covered with the snows of centuries.

"Tobacco was among the products of this elevated region; yet the Peruvians used it only for medicinal purposes. They may have found a substitute for its narcotic qualities in the coca... (they made) a preparation for chewing, much like the betel-leaf of the East".

5 - Peruvian Sheep - Great Hunts - Manufactures - Mechanical skill - Architecture - Concluding reflections.

A nation which had made such progress in agriculture might be reasonably expected to have made, also, some proficiency in the mechanical arts,—especially when, as in the case of the Peruvians, their agricultural economy demanded in itself no inconsiderable degree of mechanical skill. Among most nations, progress in manufactures has been found to have an intimate connection with the progress of husbandry. Both arts are directed to the same great object of supplying the necessaries, the comforts, or, in a more refined condition of society, the luxuries of life; and when the one is brought to a perfection that infers a certain advance in civilization, the other must naturally find a corresponding development under the increasing demands and capacities of such a state. The subjects of the Incas, in their patient and tranquil devotion to the more humble occupations of industry which bound them to their native soil, bore greater resemblance to the Oriental nations, as the Hindoos and Chinese, than they bore to the members of the great Anglo-Saxon family, whose hardy temper has driven them to seek their fortunes on the stormy ocean, and to open a commerce with the most distant regions of the globe. The Peruvians, though lining a long extent of sea-coast, had no foreign commerce.

They had peculiar advantages for domestic manufacture in a material incomparably superior to anything possessed by the other races of the Western continent. They found a good substitute for linen in a fabric which, like the Aztecs, they knew how to weave from the tough thread of the maguey. Cotton grew luxuriantly on the low, sultry level of the coast, and furnished them with a clothing suitable to the milder latitudes of the country. But from the llama and the kindred species of Peruvian sheep they obtained a fleece adapted to the colder climate of the table-land, "more estimable", to quote the language of a well-informed writer, "than the down of the Canadian beaver, the fleece of the *brebis des Calmoucks,* or of the Syrian goat".

Of the four varieties of the Peruvian sheep, the llama, the one most familiarly known, is the least valuable on account of its wool. It is chiefly employed as a beast of burden, for which, although it is somewhat larger than any of the other varieties, its diminutive size and strength would seem to disqualify it. It carries a load of little more than a hundred pounds, and cannot travel above three or four leagues in a day. But all this is compensated by the little care and cost required for its management and its maintenance. It picks up an easy subsistence from the moss and stunted herbage that grow scantily along the withered sides and the steeps of the Cordilleras. The structure of its stomach, like that of the camel, is such as to enable it to dispense with any supply of water for weeks, nay, months together. Its spongy hoof, armed with a claw or pointed talon to enable it to take secure hold on the ice, never requires to be shod; and the load laid upon its back rests securely in its bed of wool, without the aid of girth or saddle. The llamas move in troops of five hundred or even a thousand, and thus, though each individual carries but little, the aggregate is considerable. The whole caravan travels on at its regular pace, passing the night in the open air without suffering from the coldest temperature, and marching in perfect order, and in obedience to the voice of the driver. It is only when overloaded that the spirited little animal refuses to stir, and neither blows nor caresses can induce him to rise from the ground. He is as sturdy in asserting his rights on this occasion, as he is usually docile and unresisting.

The employment of domestic animals distinguished the Peruvians from the other races of the New World. This economy of human labor by the substitution of the brute is an important element of civilization, inferior only to what is gained by the substitution of machinery for both. Yet the ancient Peruvians seem to have made much less account of it than their Spanish conquerors, and to have valued the llama, in common with the other animals of that genus, chiefly for its fleece. Immense herds of these "large cattle", as they were called, and of the "smaller cattle", or *alpacas*, were held by the government, as already noticed, and placed under the direction of shepherds, who conducted them from one quarter of the country to another, according to the changes of the season. These migrations were regulated with all the precision with which the code of the *mesta* determined the migrations of the vast merino flocks in Spain; and the Conquerors, when they landed in Peru, were amazed at finding a race of animals so similar to their own in properties and habits, and under the control of a system of legislation which might seem to have been imported from their native land.

But the richest store of wool was obtained, not from these domesticated animals, but from the two other species, the *huanacos* and the *vicuñas,* which roamed in native freedom over the frozen ranges of the Cordilleras; where not unfrequently they might be seen scaling the snow-covered peaks which no living thing inhabits save the condor, the huge bird of the Andes, whose broad pinions bear him up in the atmosphere to the height of more than twenty thousand feet above the level of the sea. In these rugged pastures, "the flock without a fold" finds sufficient sustenance in the *ychu,* a species of grass which is found scattered all along the great ridge of the Cordilleras, from the equator to the southern limits of Patagonia. And as these limits define the territory traversed by the Peruvian sheep, which rarely, if ever, venture north of the line, it seems not improbable that this mysterious little plant is so important to their existence, that the absence of it is the principal reason why they have not penetrated to the northern latitudes of Quito and New Granada.

But, although thus roaming without a master over the boundless wastes of the Cordilleras, the Peruvian peasant was never allowed to hunt these wild animals, which were protected by laws as severe as were the sleek herds that grazed on the more cultivated slopes of the plateau. The wild game of the forest and the mountain was as much the property of the government, as if it had been inclosed within a park, or penned within a fold. It was only on stated occasions, at the great hunts, which took place once a year, under the personal superintendence of the Inca or his principal officers, that the game was allowed to be taken. These hunts were not repeated in the same quarter of the country oftener than once in four years, that time might be allowed for the waste occasioned by them to be replenished. At the appointed time, all those living in the district and its neighborhood, to the number, it might be, of fifty or sixty thousand men, were distributed round, so as to form a cordon of immense extent, that should embrace the whole country which was to be hunted over. The men were armed with long poles and spears, with which they beat up game of every description lurking in the woods, the valleys, and the mountains, killing the beasts of prey without mercy, and driving the others, consisting chiefly of the deer of the country, and the huanacos and vicuñas, towards the centre of the wide-extended circle; until, as this gradually contracted, the timid inhabitants of

"The employment of domestic animals distinguished the Peruvians from the other races of the new world": upon the lid of a vase of the time, a peasant playing the flute leads a llama

(Musée de l'Homme, Paris).—"The Peruvians produced an article of great strength and durability by mixing the hair of animals with wool".

the forest were concentrated on some spacious plain, where the eye of the hunter might range freely over his victims, who found no place for shelter or escape.

The male deer and some of the coarser kind of the Peruvian sheep were slaughtered; their skins were reserved for the various useful manufactures to which they are ordinarily applied, and their flesh, cut into thin slices, was distributed among the people, who converted it into *charqui,* the dried meat of the country, which constituted then the sole, as it has since the principal, animal food of the lower classes of Peru.

But nearly the whole of the sheep, amounting usually to thirty or forty thousand, or even a larger number, after being carefully sheared, were suffered to escape and regain their solitary haunts among the mountains. The wool thus collected was deposited in the royal magazines, whence, in due time, it was dealt out to the people. The coarser quality was worked up into garments for their own use, and the finer for the Inca; for none but an Inca noble could wear the fine fabric of the vicuña.

The Peruvians showed great skill in the manufacture of different articles for the royal household from this delicate material, which, under the name of *vigonia* wool, is now familiar to the looms of Europe. It was wrought into shawls, robes, and other articles of dress for the monarch, and into carpets, coverlets, and hangings for the imperial palaces and the temples. The cloth was finished on both sides alike; the delicacy of the texture was such as to give it the lustre of silk; and the brilliancy of the dyes excited the admiration and the envy of the European artisan. The Peruvians produced also an article of great strength and durability by mixing the hair of animals with wool; and they were expert in the beautiful feather-work, which they held of less account than the

107

Mexicans from the superior quality of the materials for other fabrics, which they had at their command.

The natives showed a skill in other mechanical arts similar to that displayed by their manufactures of cloth. Every man in Peru was expected to be acquainted with the various handicrafts essential to domestic comfort. No long apprenticeship was required for this, where the wants were so few as among the simple peasantry of the Incas. But it this were all, it would imply but a very moderate advancement in the arts. There were certain individuals, however, carefully trained to those occupations which minister to the demands of the more opulent classes of society. These occupations, like every other calling and office in Peru, always descended from father to son. The division of castes, in this particular, was as precise as that which existed in Egypt or Hindostan. If this arrangement be unfavorable to originality, or to the development of the peculiar talent of the individual, it as least conduces to an easy and finished execution by familiarizing the artist with the practice of his art from childhood.

The royal magazines and the *huacas* or tombs of the Incas have been found to contain many specimens of curious and elaborate workmanship. Among these are vases of gold and silver, bracelets, collars, and other ornaments for the person; utensils of every description, some of fine clay, and many more of copper; mirrors of a hard, polished stone, or burnished silver, with a great variety of other articles made frequently on a whimsical pattern, evincing quite as much ingenuity as taste or inventive talent. The character of the Peruvian mind led to imitation, in fact, rather than invention, to delicacy and minuteness of finish, rather than to boldness or beauty of design.

That they should have accomplished these difficult works with such tools as they

"The character of the Peruvian mind led to imitation rather than invention, to delicacy and minuteness of finish, rather than to boldness or beauty of design".—Opposite left: decoration of a vase from the southern coast of Peru; below: a warrior holding the tail of a fantastic animal and threatening it with an axe.

Right: decoration around another vase. Below, double vase: each figure holds a vessel in his hands (region of Cuzco).

Two vases made of metal with decorations in repoussé work.

possessed, is truly wonderful. It was comparatively easy to cast and even to sculpture metallic substances, both of which they did with consummate skill. But that they should have shown the like facility in cutting the hardest substances, as emeralds and other precious stones, is not so easy to explain. Emeralds they obtained in considerable quantity from the barren district of Atacames, and this inflexible material seems to have been almost as ductile in the hands of the Peruvian artist as if it had been made of clay. Yet the natives were unacquainted with the use of iron, though the soil was largely impregnated with it. The tools used were of stone, or more frequently of copper. But the material on which they relied for the execution of their most difficult tasks was formed by combining a very small portion of tin with copper. This composition gave a hardness to the metal which seems to have been little inferior to that of steel. With the aid of it, not only did the Peruvian artisan hew into shape porphyry and granite, but by his patient industry accomplished works which the European would not have ventured to undertake. Among the remains of the monuments of Cannar may be seen movable rings in the muzzles of animals, all nicely sculptured of one entire block of granite. It is worthy of remark, that the Egyptians, the Mexicans, and the Peruvians, in their progress towards civilization, should never have detected the use of iron, which lay around them in abundance; and that they should each, without any knowledge of the other, have found a substitute for it in such a curious composition of metals as gave to their tools almost the temper of steel; a secret that has been lost—or, to speak more correctly, has never been discovered—by the civilized European.

I have already spoken of the large quantity of gold and silver wrought into various articles of elegance and utility for the Incas; though the amount was inconsiderable, in comparison with what could have been afforded by the mineral riches of the land, and with what has since been obtained by the more sagacious and unscrupulous cupidity of the white man. God was gathered by the Incas from the deposits of the streams. They extracted the ore also in considerable quantities from the valley of Curimayo, northeast of Caxamarca, as well as from other places; and the silver mines of Porco, in particular, yielded them considerable returns. Yet they did not attempt to penetrate into the bowels of the earth by sinking a shaft, but simply excavated a cavern in the steep sides of the mountain, or, at most, opened a horizonal vein of moderate depth. They were equally deficient in the knowledge of the best means of detaching the precious metal from the dross with which it was united, and had no idea of the virtues of quicksilver,—a mineral not rare in Peru,—as an amalgam to effect this decomposition. Their method of smelting the ore was by means of furnaces built in elevated and exposed situations, where they might be fanned by the strong breezes of the mountains. The subjects of the Incas, in short, with all their patient perseverance, did little more than penetrate below the crust, the outer rind, as it were, formed over those golden caverns which lie hidden in the dark depths of the Andes. Yet what they gleaned from the surface was more than adequate for all their demands. For they were not a commercial people, and had no knowledge of money. In this they differed from the ancient Mexicans, who had an established currency of a determinate value. In one respect, however, they were superior to their American rivals, since they made use of weights to determine the quantity of their commodities, a thing wholly unknown to the Aztecs. This fact is ascertained by the discovery of silver balances, adjusted with perfect accuracy, in some of the tombs of the Incas.

But the surest test of the civilization of a people—at least, as sure as any— afforded by mechanical art is to be found in their architecture, which presents so noble a field for the display of the grand and the beautiful, and which, at the same time, is so intimately connected with the essential comforts of life. There is no object on which the resources of the wealthy are more freely lavished, or which calls out more effectually the inventive talent of the artist. The painter and the sculptor may display their individual taste and magnificence that are stamped in a peculiar manner by the genius of the nation. The Greek, the Egyptian, the Saracen, the Gothic,—what a key do their respective styles afford to the character and condition of the people! The monuments of China, of Hindostan, and of Central America are all indicative of an immature period, in which the imagination has not been disciplined by study, and which, therefore, in its best results, betrays only the ill-regulated aspirations after the beautiful, that belong to a semi-civilized people.

The Peruvian architecture, bearing also the general characteristics of an imperfect state of refinement, had still its peculiar character; and so uniform was that character, that the edifices throughout the country seem to have been all cast in the same mould. They were usually built of porphyry or granite; not unfrequently of brick. This, which was formed into blocks or squares of much larger dimensions than our brick, was made of a tenacious earth mixed up with reeds or tough grass, and acquired a degree of hardness with age that made it insensible alike to the storms and the more trying sun of the tropics. The walls were of great thickness, but low, seldom reaching to more than twelve or fourteen feet in height. It is rare to meet with accounts of a building that rose to a second story.

"The doorways were made with the sides approaching each other towards the top, so that the lintel was considerably narrower than the threshold, a peculiarity, also, in Egyptian architecture".

The apartments had no communication with one another, but usually opened into a court; and, as they were unprovided with windows, or apertures that served for them, the only light from without must have been admitted by the doorways. These were made with the sides approaching each other towards the top, so that the lintel was considerably narrower than the threshold, a peculiarity, also, in Egyptian architecture. The roofs have for the most part disappeared with time. Some few survive in the less ambitious edifices, of a singular bell-shape, and made of a composition of earth and pebbles. They are supposed, however, to have been generally formed of more perishable materials, of wood or straw. It is certain that some of the most considerable stone-buildings were thatched with straw. Many seem to have been constructed without the aid of cement; and writers have contended that the Peruvians were unacquainted with the use of mortar, or cement of any kind. But a close, tenacious mould, mixed with lime, may be discovered filling up the interstices of the granite in some buildings; and in others, where the well-fitted blocks leave no room for this coarser material, the eye of the antiquary has detected a fine bituminous glue, as hard as the rock itself.

The greatest simplicity is observed in the construction of the buildings, which are usually free from outward ornament; though in some the huge stones are shaped into a convex form with great regularity, and adjusted with such nice precision to one another, that it would be impossible, but for the flutings, to determine the line of junction. In others, the stone is rough, as it was taken from the quarry, in the most irregular forms, with the edges nicely wrought and fitted to each other. There is no appearance of columns or of arches; though there is some contradiction as to the latter point. But it is not to be doubted, that, although they may have made some approach to this mode of construction by the greater or less inclination of the walls, the Peruvian architects were wholly unacquainted with the true principle of the circular arch reposing one its key-stone.

The architecture of the Incas is characterized, says an eminent traveller, "by simplicity, symmetry, and solidity". It may seem unphilosophical to condemn the peculiar fashion of a nation as indicating want of taste, because its standard of taste differs from our own. Yet there is an incongruity in the composition of the Peruvian buildings which argues a very imperfect acquaintance with the first principles of architecture. While they put together their bulky masses of porphyry and granite with the nicest art, they were incapable of mortising their timbers, and, in their ignorance of iron, knew no better way of holding the beams together that tying them with thongs of maguey. In the same incongruous spirit, the building that was thatched with straw, and unilluminated by a window, was glowing with tapestries of gold and

"Many edifices seem to have been constructed without the aid of cement"—Below: assembling of monoliths in the fortress of Cuzco.

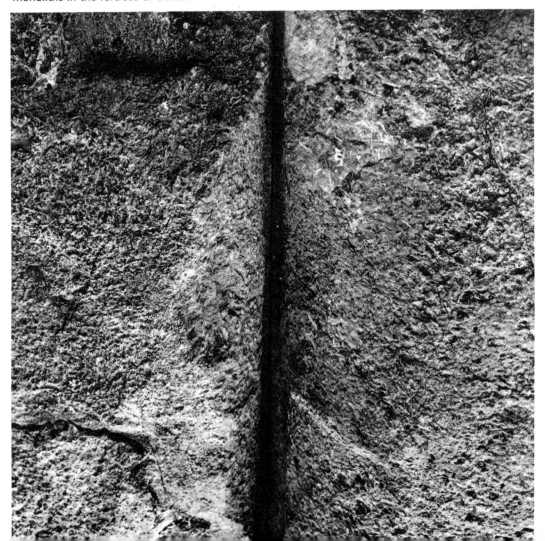

silver! These are the inconsistencies of a rude people, among whom the arts are but partially developed. It might not be difficult to find examples of like inconsistency in the architecture and domestic arrangements of our Anglo-Saxon, and, at a still later period of our Norman ancestors.

Yet the buildings of the Incas were accommodated to the character of the climate, and were well fitted to resist those terrible convulsions which belong to the land of volcanoes. The wisdom of their plan is attested by the number which still survive, while the more modern constructions of the Conquerors have been buried in ruins. The hand of the Conquerors, indeed, has fallen heavily on these venerable monuments, and, in their blind and superstitious search for hidden treasure, has caused infinitely more ruin than time or the earthquake. Yet enough of these monuments still remain to invite the researches of the antiquary. Those only in the most conspicuous situations have been hitherto examined. But, by the testimony of travellers, many more are to be found in the less frequented parts of the country; and we may hope they will one day call forth a kindred spirit of enterprise to that which has so successfully explored the mysterious recesses of Central America and Yucatan.

I cannot close this analysis of the Peruvian institutions without a few reflections on their general character and tendency, which, if they involve some repetition of previous remarks, may, I trust, be excused, from my desire to leave a correct and consistent impression on the reader. In this survey, we cannot but be struck with the total dissimilarity between these institutions and those of the Aztecs,—the other great nation who led in the march of civilization on this western continent, and whose empire in the northern portion of it was as conspicuous as that of the Incas in the south. Both nations came on the plateau, and commenced their career of conquest, at dates, it may be, not far removed from each other. And it is worthy of notice, that, in America, the elevated region along the crests of the great mountain ranges should have been the chosen seat of civilization in both hemispheres.

Very different was the policy pursued by the two races in their military career. The Aztecs, animated by the most ferocious spirit, carried on a war of extermination, signalizing their triumphs by the sacrifice of hecatombs of captives; while the Incas, although they pursued the game of conquest with equal pertinacity, preferred a milder policy, substituting negotiation and intrigue for violence, and dealt with their antagonists so that their future resources should not be crippled, and that they should come as friends, not as foes, into the bosom of the empire.

Their policy toward the conquered forms a contrast no less striking to that pursued by the Aztecs. The Mexican vassals were ground by excessive imposts and military conscriptions. No regard was had to their welfare, and the only limit to oppression was the power of endurance. They were overawed by fortresses and armed garrisons, and were made to feel every hour that they were not part and parcel of the nation, but held only in subjugation as a conquered people. The Incas, on the other hand, admitted their new subjects at once to all the rights enjoyed by the rest of the community; and, though they made them conform to the established laws and usages of the empire, they watched over their personal security and comfort with a sort of parental solicitude. The motley population, thus bound together by common interest, was animated by a common feeling of loyalty, which gave greater strength and stability to the empire, as it became more and more widely extended; while the various tribes who successively came under the

Mexican sceptre, being held together only by the pressure of external force, were ready to fall asunder the moment that that force was withdrawn. The policy of the two nations displayed the principle of fear as contrasted with the principle of love.

The characteristic features of their religious systems had as little resemblance to each other. The whole Aztec pantheon partook more or less of the sanguinary spirit of the terrible war-god who presided over it, and their frivolous ceremonial almost always terminated with human sacrifice and cannibal orgies. But the rites of the Peruvians were of a more innocent cast, as they tended to a more spiritual worship. For the worship of the Creator is most nearly approached by that of the heavenly bodies, which, as they revolve in their bright orbits, seem to be the most glorious symbols of his beneficence and power.

In the minuter mechanical arts, both showed considerable skill; but in the construction of important public works, of roads, aqueducts, canals, and in agriculture in all its details, the Peruvians were much superior. Strange that they should have fallen so far below their rivals in their efforts after a higher intellectual culture, in astronomical science, more especially, and in the art of communicating thought by visible symbols. When we consider the greater refinement of the Incas, their inferiority to the Aztecs in these particulars can be explained only by the fact, that the latter in all probability were indebted for their science to the race who preceded them in the land,—that shadowy race whose origin and whose end are alike veiled from the eye of the inquirer, but who possibly may have sought a refuge from their ferocious invaders in those regions of Central America the architectural remains of which now supply us with the most pleasing monuments of Indian civilization. It is with this more polished race, to whom the Peruvians seem to have borne some resemblance in their mental and moral organization, that they should be compared. Had the empire of the Incas been permitted to extend itself with the rapid strides with which it was advancing at the period of the Spanish conquest, the two races might have come into conflict, or, perhaps, into alliance with one another.

The Mexicans and Peruvians, so different in the character of their peculiar civilization, were, it seems probable, ignorant of each other's existence; and it may appear singular, that, during the simultaneous continuance of their empires, some of the seeds of science and of art, which pass so imperceptibly from one people to another, should not have found their way across the interval which separated the two nations. They furnish an interesting example of the opposite directions which the human mind may take in its struggle to emerge from darkness into the light of civilization.

A closer resemblance—as I have more than once taken occasion to notice—may be found between the Peruvian institutions and some of the despotic governments of Eastern Asia; those governments where despotism appears in its more mitigated form, and the whole people, under the patriarchal sway of its sovereign, seem to be gathered together like the members of one vast family. Such were the Chinese, for example, whom the Peruvians resembled in their implicit obedience to authority, their mild yet somewhat stubborn temper, their solicitude for forms, their reverence for ancient usage, their skill in the minuter manufactures, their imitative rather than inventive cast of mind, and their invincible patience, which serves instead of a more adventurous spirit for the execution of difficult undertakings.

A still closer analogy may be found with the natives of Hindostan in their division into

castes, their worship of the heavenly bodies and the elements of nature, and their acquaintance with the scientific principles of husbandry. To the ancient Egyptians, also, they bore considerable resemblance in the same particulars, as well as in those ideas of a future existence which led them to attach so much importance to the permanent preservation of the body.

But we shall look in vain in the history of the East for a parallel to the absolute control exercised by the Incas over their subjects. In the East, this was founded on physical power,—on the external resources of the government. The authority of the Inca might be compared with that of the Pope in the day of his might, when Christendom trembled at the thunders of the Vatican, and the successor of St. Peter set his foot on the necks of princes. But the authority of the Pope was founded on opinion. His temporal power was nothing. The empire of the Incas rested on both. It was a theocracy more potent in its operation than that of the Jews; for, though the sanction of the law might be as great among the latter, the law was expounded by a human lawgiver, the servant and representative of Divinity. But the Inca was both the lawgiver and the law. He was not merely the representative of Divinity, or, like the Pope, its vicegerent, but he was Divinity itself. The violation of his ordinance was sacrilege. Never was there a scheme of government enforced by such terrible sanctions, or which bore so oppressively on the subjects of it. For it reached not only to the visible acts, but to the private conduct, the words, the very thoughts, of its vassals.

The admirable remains of the city of Machu-Picchu were not known at the time of William Prescott. They were only discovered in 1912 but the study of this impressive site added nothing new to what Prescott had established; on the contrary, these ruins constitute a brilliant illustration of his work.

It added not a little to the efficacy of the government, that, below the sovereign, there was an order of hereditary nobles of the same divine original with himself, who, placed far below himself, were still immeasurably above the rest of the community, not merely by descent, but, as it would seem, by their intellectual nature. These were the exclusive depositaries of power, and, as their long hereditary training made them familiar with their vocation, and secured them implicit deference from the multitude, they became the prompt and well-practised agents for carrying out the executive measures of the administration. All that occurred throughout the wide extent of his empire—such was the perfect system of communication—passed in review, as it were, before the eyes of the monarch, and a thousand hands, armed with irresistible authority, stood ready in every quarter to do his bidding. Was it not, as we have said, the most oppressive, though the mildest, of despotisms?

It was the mildest, from the very circumstance, that the transcendent rank of the sovereign, and the humble, nay, superstitious, devotion to his will made it superfluous to assert this will by acts of violence or rigor. The great mass of the people may have appeared to his eyes as but little removed above the condition of the brute, formed to minister to his pleasures. But, from their very helplessness, he regarded them with feelings of commiseration, like those which a kind master might feel for the poor animals committed to his charge, or—to do justice to the beneficent character attributed to many of the Incas—that a parent might feel for his young and impotent offspring. The laws were carefully directed to their preservation and personal comfort. The people were not allowed to be employed on works pernicious to their health, nor to pine—a sad contrast to their subsequent destiny—under the imposi-

The representation of human figure, under aspects which would be considered to-day as most "modern", was essentially the object of pottery decoration!

Left: figure with flute, painted on a vase.
Opposite: the very shape of the vase evokes the human figures, with striking truthfulness.
Above; some kind of superadded caricature (Musée de l'Homme).

Left: A doorway of the circular temple of Machu Picchu overlooking the sides of the mountain.

Right: Observatory, with the gnomon.

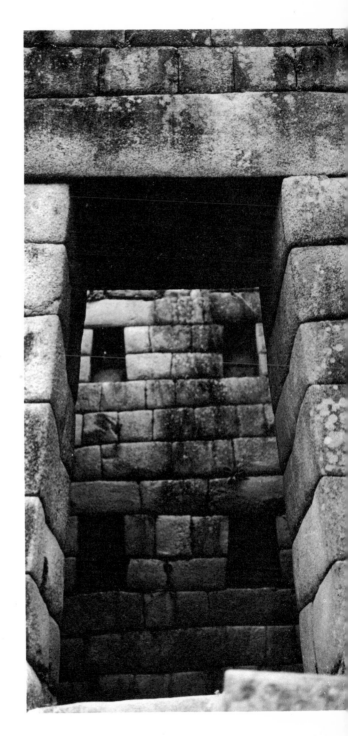

Left: Stone of sacrifice, in front of the remains of the palace of Machu-Picchu.—Right: doorway of an out-building of the circular temple of Machu-Picchu, opening on to what certain authors call "the princesses'apartments".

tion of tasks too heavy for their powers. They were never made the victims of public or private extortion; and a benevolent forecast watched carefully over their necessities, and provided for their relief in seasons of infirmity, and for their sustenance in health. The government of the Incas, however arbitrary in form, was in its spirit truly patriarchal.

Yet in this there was nothing cheering to the dignity of human nature. What the people had was conceded as a boon, not as a right. When a nation was brought under the sceptre of the Incas, it resigned every personal right, even the rights dearest to humanity. Under this extraordinary polity, a people advanced in many of the social refinements, well skilled in manufactures and agriculture, were unacquainted, as we have seen, with money. They had nothing that deserved to be called property. They could follow no craft, could engage in no labor, no amusement, but such as was specially provided by law. They could not change their residence or their dress without a license from the government. They could not even exercise the freedom which is conceded to the most abject in other countries, that of selecting their own wives. The imperative spirit of despotism would not allow them to be happy or miserable in any way but that established by law. The power of free agency—the inestimable and inborn right of every human being—was annihilated in Peru.

The astonishing mechanism of the Peruvian polity could have resulted only from the combined authority of opinion and positive power in the ruler to an extent unprecedented in the history of man. Yet that it should have so successfully gone into operation, and so long endured, in opposition to the taste, the prejudices, and the very principles of our nature, is a strong proof of a generally wise and temperate administration of the government.

The policy habitually pursued by the Incas for the *prevention* of evils that might have disturbed the order of things is well exemplified in their provisions against poverty and idleness. In these they rightly discerned the two great causes of disaffection in a populous community. The industry of the people was secured not only by their compulsory occupations at home, but by their employment on those great public works which covered every part of the country, and which still bear testimony in their decay to their primitive grandeur. Yet it may well astonish us to find, that the natural difficulty of these undertakings, sufficiently great in itself, considering the imperfection of their tools and machinery, was inconceivably enhanced by the politic contrivance of government. The royal edifices of Quito, we are assured by the Spanish conquerors, were constructed of huge masses of stone, many of which were carried all the way along the mountain roads from Cuzco, a distance of several hundred leagues. The great square of the capital was filled to a considerable depth with mould brought with incredible labor up the steep slopes of the Cordilleras from the distant shores of the Pacific Ocean. Labor was regarded not only as a means, but as an end, by the Peruvian law .

With their manifold provisions against poverty the reader has already been made acquainted. They were so perfect, that, in their wide extent of territory,—much of it smitten with the curse of barrenness,—no man, however humble, suffered from the want of food and clothing. Famine, so common a scourge in every other American nation, so common at that period in every country of civilized Europe, was an evil unknown in the dominions of the Incas.

The most enlightened of the Spaniards who first visited Peru, struck with the general appearance of plenty and prosperity, and with the astonishing order with which every thing throughout the country was regulated, are loud in their expressions of admiration. No

"The buildings of the Incas were accomodated to the character of the climate... The wisdom of their plan is attested by the number which still survive"—(Remains of the "military quarter" of Machu-Picchu).

better government, in their opinion, could have been devised for the people. Contented with their condition, and free from vice, to borrow the language of an eminent authority of that early day, the mild and docile character of the Peruvians would have well fitted them to receive the teachings of Christianity, had the love of conversion, instead of gold, animated the breasts of the Conquerors. And a philosopher of a later time, warmed by the contemplation of the picture—which his own fancy had colored—of public prosperity and private happiness under the rule of the Incas, pronounces "the *moral* man in Peru far superior to the European".

Yet such results are scarcely reconcilable with the theory of the government I have attempted to analyze. Where there is no free agency, there can be no morality. Where there is no temptation, there can be little claim to virtue. Where the routine is rigorously prescribed by law, the law, and not the man, must have the credit of the conduct. If that government is the best, which is felt the least, which encroaches on the natural liberty of the subject only so far as is essential to civil subordination, then of all governments devised by man the Peruvian has the least real claim to our admiration.

It is not easy to comprehend the genius and the full import of institutions so opposite to those of our own free republic, where every man, however humble his condition, may aspire to the highest honors of the state,—may select his own career, and carve out his fortune in his own way; where the light of

125

knowledge, instead of being concentrated on a chosen few, is shed abroad like the light of day, and suffered to fall equally on the poor and the rich; where the collision of man with man wakens a generous emulation that calls out latent talent and tasks the energies to the utmost; where consciousness of independence gives a feeling of self-reliance unknown to the timid subjects of despotism; where, in short, the government is made for man,—not as in Peru, where man seemed to be made only for the government. The New World is the theatre in which these two political systems, so opposite in their character, have been carried into operation. The empire of the Incas has passed away and left no trace. The other great experiment is still going on,—the experiment which is to solve the problem, so long contested in the Old World, of the capacity of man for self-government. Alas for humanity, if it should fail!

The testimony of the Spanish conquerors is not uniform in respect to the favorable influence exerted by the Peruvian institutions on the character of the people. Drinking and dancing are said to have been the pleasures to which they were immoderately addicted. Like the slaves and serfs in other lands, whose position excluded them from more serious and ennobling occupations, they found a substitute in frivolous or sensual indulgence. Lazy, luxurious, and licentious, are the epithets bestowed on them by one of those who saw them at the Conquest, but whose pen was not too friendly to the Indian. Yet the spirit of independence could hardly be strong in a people who had no interest in the soil, no personal rights to defend; and the facility with which they yielded to the Spanish invader—after every allowance for their comparative inferiority—argues a deplorable destitution of that patriotic feeling which holds life as little in comparison with freedom.

But we must not judge too hardly of the unfortunate native, because he quailed before the civilization of the European. We must not be insensible to the really great results that were achieved by the government of the Incas. We must not forget, that, under their rule, the meanest of the people enjoyed a far greater degree of personal comfort, at least, a greater exemption from physical suffering, than was possessed by similar classes in other nations on the American continent,—greater, probably, than was possessed by these classes in most of the countries of feudal Europe. Under their sceptre, the higher orders of the state had made advances in many of the arts that belong to a cultivated community. The foundations of a regular government were laid, which, in an age of rapine, secured to its subjects the inestimable blessings of tranquillity and safety. By the well-sustained policy of the Incas, the rude tribes of the forest were gradually drawn from their fastnesses, and gathered within the folds of civilization; and of these materials was constructed a flourishing and populous empire, such as was to be found in no other quarter of the American continent. The defects of this government were those of over-refinement in legislation,—the last defects to have been looked for, certainly, in the American aborigines.

Opposite: design of a Peruvian cloth of the time.

Appendix - Index

Left: Design of a cloth of the time.
Below: This decoration on a vase shows a warrior leading a prisoner.

Cuzco, at the time of the Incas, by Th. de Bry.

I have not thought it necessary to swell this Introduction by an inquiry into the origin of Peruvian civilization, like that appended to the history of the Mexican. The Peruvian history doubtless suggests analogies with more than one nation in the East, some of which have been briefly adverted to in the preceding pages; although these analogies are adduced there not as evidence of a common origin, but as showing the coincidences which might naturally spring up among different nations under the same phase of civilization. Such coincidences are neither so numerous nor so striking as those afforded by the Aztec history. The correspondence presented by the astronomical science of the Mexicans is alone of more importance than all the rest. Yet the light of analogy, afforded by the institutions of the Incas, seems to point, as far as it goes, towards the same direction; and as the investigation could present but little substantially to confirm, and still less to confute, the views taken in the former disquisition, I have not thought it best to fatigue the reader with it.

Two of the prominent authorities on whom I have relied in this Introductory portion of the work, are Juan de Sarmiento and the Licentiate Ondegardo. Of the former I have been able to collect no information beyond what is afforded by this own writings. In the title prefixed to his manuscript, he is styled President of the Council of the Indies, a post of high authority, which infers a weight of character in the party, and means of information, that entitle his opinions on colonial topics to great deference.

130

These means of information were much enlarged by Sarmiento's visit to the colonies, during the administration of Gasca. Having conceived the design of compiling a history of the ancient Peruvian institutions, he visited Cuzco, as he tells us, in 1550, and there drew from the natives themselves the materials for his narrative. His position gave him access to the most authentic sources of knowledge, and from the lips of the Inca nobles, the best instructed of the conquered race, he gathered the traditions of their national history and institutions. The quipus formed, as we have seen, an imperfect system of mnemonics, requiring constant attention, and much inferior to the Mexican hieroglyphics. It was only by diligent instruction that they were made available to historical purposes; and this instruction was so far neglected after the Conquest, that the ancient annals of the country would have perished with the generation which was the sole depositary of them, had it not been for the efforts of a few intelligent scholars, like Sarmiento, who saw the importance, at this critical period, of cultivating an intercourse with the natives, and drawing from them their hidden stores of information.

To give still further authenticity to his work, Sarmiento travelled over the country, examined the principal objects of interest with his own eyes, and thus verified the accounts of the natives as far as possible by personal observation. The result of these labors was his work entitled, "Relacion de la sucesion y govierno de las Yngas Señores naturales que fueron de las Provincias del Peru y otras cosas tocantes á aquel Reyno, para el Iltmo. Señor D Juan Sarmiento, Presidente del Consejo R[l] de Indias".

It is divided into chapters, and embraces about four hundred folio pages in manuscript. The introductory portion of the work is occupied with the traditionary tales of the origin and early period of the Incas; teeming, as usual, in the antiquities of a barbarous people, with legendary fables of the most wild and monstrous character. Yet these puerile conceptions afford an inexhaustible mine for the labors of the antiquarian, who endeavors

Childhood, at the time of the Incas: costume of a little boy, five or seven years old.—A nobleman and his son.

132

to unravel the allegorical web which a cunning priesthood had devised as symbolical of those mysteries of creation that it was beyond their power to comprehend. But Sarmiento happily confines himself to the mere statement of traditional fables, without the chimerical ambition to explain them.

From this region of romance, Sarmiento passes to the institutions of the Peruvians, describes their ancient polity, their religion, their progress in the arts, especially agriculture; and presents, in short, an elaborate picture of the civilization which they reached under the Inca dynasty. This part of his work, resting, as it does, on the best authority, confirmed in many instances by his own observations, is of unquestionable value, and is written with an apparent respect for truth, that engages the confidence of the reader. The concluding portion of the manuscript is occupied with the civil history of the country. The reigns of the early Incas, which lie beyond the sober province of history, he despatches with commendable brevity. But on the three last reigns, and fortunately of the greatest

princes who occupied the Peruvian throne, he is more diffuse. This was comparatively firm ground for the chronicler, for the events were too recent to be obscured by the vulgar legends that gather like moss round every incident of the older time. His account stops with the Spanish invasion; for this story, Sarmiento felt, might be safely left to his contemporaries who acted a part in it, but whose taste and education had qualified them but indifferently for exploring the antiquities and social institutions of the natives.

Sarmiento's work is composed in a simple, perspicuous style, without that ambition of rhetorical display too common with his countrymen. He writes with honest candor, and while he does ample justice to the merits and capacity of the conquered races, he notices with indignation the atrocities of the Spaniards and the demoralizing tendency of the Conquest. It may be thought, indeed, that he forms too high an estimate of the attainments of the nation under the Incas. And it is not improbable, that, astonished by the vestiges it afforded of an original civilization,

133

he became enamoured of his subject, and thus exhibited it in colors somewhat too glowing to the eye of the European. But this was an amiable failing, not too largely shared by the stern Conquerors, who subverted the institutions of the country, and saw little to admire in it, save its gold. It must be further admitted, that Sarmiento has no design to impose on his reader, and that he is careful to distinguish between what he reports on hearsay, and what on personal experience. The Father of History himself does not discriminate between these two things more carefully.

Neither is the Spanish historian to be altogether vindicated from the superstition which belongs to his time; and we often find him referring to the immediate interposition of Satan those effects which might quite as well be charged on the perverseness of man. But this was common to the age, and to the wisest men in it; and it is too much to demand of a man to be wiser than his generation. It is sufficient praise of Sarmiento, that, in an age when superstition was too often allied with fanaticism, he seems to have had no tincture of bigotry in his nature. His heart opens with benevolent fulness to the unfortunate native; and his language, while it is not kindled into the religious glow of the missionary, is warmed by a generous ray of philanthropy that embraces the conquered, no less than the conquerors, as his brethren.

Notwithstanding the great value of Sarmiento's work for the information it affords of Peru under the Incas, it is but little known, has been rarely consulted by historians, and still remains among the unpublished manuscripts which lie, like uncoined bullion, in the secret chambers of the Escurial.

The other authority to whom I have alluded, the Licentiate Polo de Ondegardo, was a highly respectable jurist, whose name appears frequently in the affairs of Peru. I find no account of the period when he first came into the country. But he was there on the arrival of Gasca, and resided at Lima under the usurpation of Gonzalo Pizarro. When the artful Cepeda endeavored to secure the signatures of the inhabitants to the instrument proclaiming the sovereignty of his chief, we

The Inca, by a Spaniard artist.

Opposite: The Inca receiving two lieutenants of Pizarro.

find Ondegardo taking the lead among those of his profession in resisting it. On Gasca's arrival, he consented to take a commission in his army. At the close of the rebellion he was made corregidor of La Plata, and subsequently of Cuzco, in which honorable station he seems to have remained several years. In the exercise of his magisterial functions, he was brought into familiar intercourse with the natives, and had ample opportunity for studying their laws and ancient customs. He conducted himself with such prudence and moderation, that he seems to have won the confidence not only of his countrymen but of the Indians; while the administration was careful to profit by his large experience in devising measures for the better government of the colony.

The *Relaciones,* so often cited in this History, were prepared at the suggestion of the viceroys, the first being addressed to the Marques de Cañete, in 1561, and the second, ten yeats later, to the Conde de Nieva. The two cover about as much ground as Sarmiento's manuscript; and the second memor-ial, written so long after the first, may be thought to intimate the advancing age of the author, in the greater carelessness and diffuseness of the composition.

As these documents are in the nature of answers to the interrogatories propounded by government, the range of topics might seem to be limited within narrower bounds than the modern historian would desire. These queries, indeed, had particular reference to the revenues, tributes,—the financial administration, in short, of the Incas; and on these obscure topics the communication of Ondegardo is particularly full. But the enlightened curiosity of government embraced a far wider range; and the answers necessarily implied an acquaintance with the domestic policy of the Incas, with their laws, social habits, their religion, science, and arts, in short, with all that make up the elements of civilization. Ondegardo's memoirs, therefore, cover the whole ground of inquiry for the philosophic historian.

In the management of these various subjects, Ondegardo displays both acuteness

The Incas and the Spaniards (continued): a provincial chief treating with a Castilian officer. Below: Pizarro received at Cuzco, from an old illustration. Good manners will not last long.

and erudition. He never shrinks from the discussion, however difficult; and while he gives his conclusions with an air of modesty, it is evident that he feels conscious of having derived his information through the most authentic channels. He rejects the fabulous with disdain; decides on the probabilities of such facts as he relates, and candidly exposes the deficiency of evidence. Far from displaying the simple enthusiasm of the well-meaning but credulous missionary, he proceeds with the cool and cautious step of a lawyer accustomed to the conflict of testimony and the uncertainty of oral tradition. This circumspect manner of proceeding, and the temperate character of his judgments, entitle Ondegardo to much higher consideration as an authority than most of his countrymen who have treated of Indian antiquities.

There runs through his writings a vein of humanity, shown particularly in his tenderness to the unfortunate natives, to whose ancient civilization he does entire, but not extravagant, justice; while, like Sarmiento, he fearlessly denounces the excesses of his own

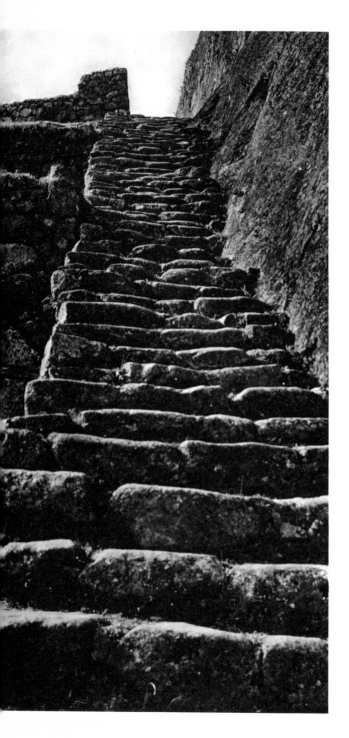

Left: Stairway at Machu-Picchu, leading to the military quarter.—View of the city: the importance of the remains as well as the grandiose aspect of the site make the city one of the most attractive places of ancient Peru.

It seems that the stones left everywhere in their country by the Incas should remain there until the end of the world or the time of an upheaval which would not be of human origin.

Right: The impressive view of the valley of Urubamba, from a terrace of Machu-Picchu.

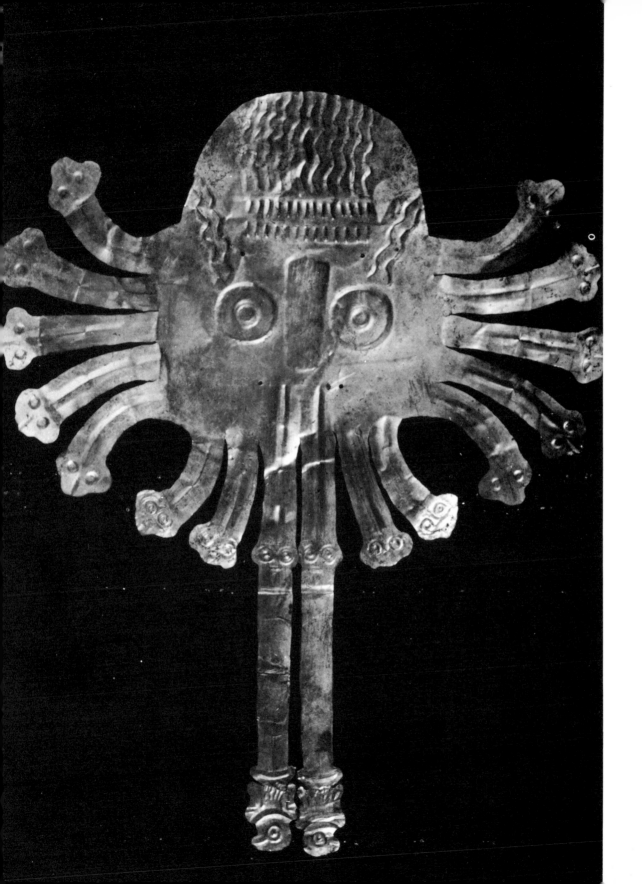

countrymen, and admits the dark reproach they had brought on the honor of the nation. But while this censure forms the strongest ground for condemnation of the Conquerors, since it comes from the lips of a Spaniard like themselves, it proves, also, that Spain in this age of violence could send forth from her bosom wise and good men who refused to make common cause with the licentious rabble around them. Indeed, proof enough is given in these very memorials of the unceasing efforts of the colonial government, from the good viceroy Mendoza downwards, to secure protection and the benefit of a mild legislation to the unfortunate natives. But the iron Conquerors, and the colonist whose heart softened only to the touch of gold, presented a formidable barrier to improvement.

Ondegardo's writings are honorably distinguished by freedom from that superstition which is the debasing characteristic of the times; a superstition shown in the easy credit given to the marvellous, and this equally whether in heathen or in Christian story; for in the former the eye of credulity could discern as readily the direct interposition of Satan, as in the latter the hand of the Almighty. It is this ready belief in a spiritual agency, whether for good or for evil, which forms one of the most prominent features in the writings of the sixteenth century. Nothing could be more repugnant to the true spirit of philosophical inquiry or more irreconcilable with rational criticism. Far from betraying such weakness, Ondegardo writes in a direct and business-like manner, estimating things for what they are worth by the plain rule of common-sense. He keeps the main object of his argument ever in view, without allowing himself, like the garrulous chroniclers of the period, to be led astray into a thousand rambling episodes that bewilder the reader and lead to nothing.

Ondegardo's memoirs deal not only with the antiquities of the nation, but with its actual condition, and with the best means for redressing the manifold evils to which it was subjected under the stern rule of its conquerors. His suggestions are replete with wisdom, and a merciful policy, that would reconcile the interests of government with the prosperity and

143

happiness of its humblest vassal. Thus, while his contemporaries gathered light from his suggestions as to the present condition of affairs, the historian of later times is no less indebted to him for information in respect to the past. His manuscript was freely consulted by Herrera and the reader, as he peruses the pages of the learned historian of the Indies, is unconsciously enjoying the benefit of the researches of Ondegardo. His valuable *Relaciones* thus had their uses for future generations, though they have never been admitted to the honors of the press. The copy in my possession, like that of Sarmiento's manuscript, for which I am indebted to that industrious bibliographer, Mr. Rich, formed part of the magnificent collection of Lord Kingsborough,—a name ever to be held in honor by the scholar for his indefatigable efforts to illustrate the antiquities of America.

Ondegardo's manuscripts, it should be remarked, do not bear his signature. But they contain allusions to several actions of the writer's life, which identify them, beyond any reasonable doubt, as his production. In the archives of Simancas is a duplicate copy of the first memorial, *Relacion Primera,* though, like the one in the Escurial, without its author's name. Muñoz assigns it to the pen of Gabriel de Rojas, a distinguished cavalier of the Conquest. This is clearly an error; for the author of the manuscript identifies himself with Ondegardo, by declaring, in his reply to the fifth interrogatory, that he was the person who discovered the mummies of the Incas in Cuzco; an act expressly referred both by Acosta and Garcilasso, to the Licentiate Polo de Ondegardo, when corregidor of that city. —Should the *savans* of Madrid hereafter embrace among the publications of valuable manuscripts these *Relaciones,* they should be careful not to be led into an error here, by the authority of a critic like Muñoz, whose criticism is rarely at fault.

Design of a tapestry (Musée de l'Homme, Paris).

Index

Figure decorating a cloth.

Index

Lower part of a hanging. (Musée de l'Homme, Paris).

Index

153

Index

154

Birds were one of the favorite designs of the Peruvian weavers.

Overleaf: These boats on lake Titicaca are quite similar to those of the Incas.

Printed in Italy